Explore the Lake District 33

Survival Guide 145

Special Features

Welcome to the Lake District

For natural splendour, nowhere in England compares to the Lake District – home to the UK's most popular national park, England's highest mountain, and a World Heritage Site since 2017. With a postcard panorama of craggy hilltops, mountain tarns and glittering lakes, it's a place that stirs the imagination. Lace up your boots: it's time to get out and explore.

Windermere (p36)

Top Sights

Windermere & the Islands

England's largest lake. **p36**

Grasmere

The beloved village of William Wordsworth, whose former home Dove Cottage (pictured) you can visit. **p52**

Hill Top

Beatrix Potter's world-famous Lakeland home. **p66**

Scafell Pike

The highest peak in England. **p112**

Holker Hall

Cumbria's answer to Downton Abbey. **p110**

JOHN MORRISON / ALAMY STOCK PHOTO ©

LEFT: JOANA KRUSE / ALAMY STOCK PHOTO ©, RIGHT: DAVID LYONS / ALAMY STOCK PHOTO ©

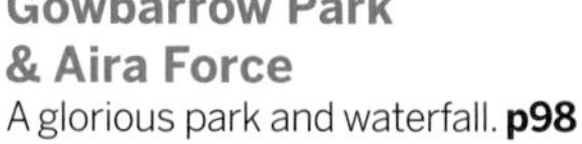

Gowbarrow Park & Aira Force

A glorious park and waterfall. **p98**

Keswick

A historic town on the gorgeous Derwentwater. **p80**

Buttermere

Arguably the loveliest of the Lakeland valleys. **p84**

Carlisle Castle

Cumbria's mightiest red-brick fortress. **p132**

Langdale Pikes

One of the classic peak-bagging hikes. **p56**

Eating

You'll eat well in the Lakes, whether it's dining in a high-class restaurant or in a cosy village inn. Sample some traditional Cumberland sausage, try Herdwick lamb or tuck into some tattie hotpot – but remember to leave room for sticky toffee pudding.

Pubs & Inns

Historic pubs and inns litter the Lakes, and they're great for getting a flavour of local life. Many feel traditional, with white-washed walls, hefty beams, slate floors and well-worn decor; others have reinvented themselves as chic, sleek gastropubs.

Restaurants

The Lake District has a good range of restaurants, from cosy village bistros to Michelin-starred wonders. The stand-out destination is L'Enclume (p122) in Cartmel, where experimental chef Simon Rogan experiments with weird and wonderful textures and ingredients.

Cafes & Tearooms

Afternoon tea is an essential post-hike ritual, and there's nearly always a convenient teashop nearby. Most Cumbrian teashops and cafes serve light lunches as well as cakes and sweet treats.

Best For Fine Dining

L'Enclume The Lake District's best (and barmiest) restaurant, bar none. (pictured; p122)

Rogan & Company Sample Simon Rogan's food without the stellar price-tag. (p122)

Lake Road Kitchen New Nordic–inspired multi-course menus in Keswick. (p46)

Old Stamp House A temple to the very best Lakeland produce. (p46)

Cottage in the Wood An out-of-the-way recommendation near Whinlatter Forest. (p92)

DAVIDCC / ALAMY STOCK PHOTO ©

Best Gastropubs

Punch Bowl Inn Is this the Lake District's top dining pub? We think so. (p45)

Drunken Duck Superb name, superb location, superb food. (p76)

Mason's Arms Cosy country pub hidden away near the pretty Lyth Valley. (p45)

Wheatsheaf Inn Much-recommended locals' pub just outside Penrith. (p143)

George & Dragon The best place for food in the Eden Valley. (p138)

Best on a Budget

Fellpack Keswick's coolest cafe, with loads of vegan and veggie options. (p81)

Great North Pie Company The British pie goes gourmet. (p47)

Apple Pie Chunky sandwiches, homemade cakes and Keswick's finest apple pie. (p46)

Lingholm Kitchen Delicious food in a delightful walled garden. (p90)

Baba Ganoush Middle Eastern and fusion flavours at this Kendal cafe. (p142)

Outdoor Activities

The Lake District is the spiritual home of English hiking (or fell walking, as it's known locally), and there are endless trails to explore, from full-day mountain treks to lowland valley rambles. But there are plenty of other outdoor pursuits on offer here too.

Fell Walking

For many people, hiking is the principal reason for a visit to the Lake District. The Lake District's most famous fell-walker, the accountant-turned-author Alfred Wainwright, recorded 214 official Lakeland fells in his seven-volume *Pictorial Guides* (he usually outlined at least two possible routes to the top or, in the case of Scafell Pike, five).

Cycling

Cycling is a great way to explore the Lake District and Cumbria, as long as you don't mind the hills. For short mountain-bike rides, the trails of Grizedale Forest (p77) and Whinlatter Forest Park (p92) are very popular.

Other Activities

Cumbria is a haven for many other outdoor activities, including rock climbing, orienteering, horse riding, archery, fell (mountain) running and ghyll (waterfall) scrambling.

Best Hard Hikes

Scafell Pike The daddy of Lakeland hikes to the top of England's highest peak. (p112)

Helvellyn A vertiginous scramble along the knife-edge ridge of Striding Edge. (p100)

Langdale Pikes The multipeak classic in Great Langdale. (p56)

Blencathra A panorama over Keswick and the northern fells. (p91)

Skiddaw A real slog, but the view is just reward. (p91)

Old Man of Coniston Steep hike through copper-mining country. (p68)

ANNA STOWE LANDSCAPES UK / ALAMY STOCK PHOTO ©

Best Easy Hikes

Catbells Derwentwater's best-loved fell, for six-year-olds and septuagenarians alike. (p91)

Hallin Fell Easy fell, massive views. (p107)

Helm Crag Tackle 'The Lion and the Lamb' near Grasmere. (p60)

Castle Crag Superb views over Borrowdale. (p91)

Loughrigg One of the best views over Grasmere. (p60)

Best Activity Companies

Rookin House Outdoor pursuits galore. (p104)

Keswick Adventure Centre Rock-climbing tuition with an indoor wall. (p81)

Platty+ Pilot a kayak on Derwentwater. (pictured; p92)

Glenridding Sailing Centre Learn to sail on Ullswater. (p105)

Hiking: Top Tip

Good walking boots, waterproof gear and, above all, a detailed map are essential items on any Lake District walk. Trails are not always easy to follow, mobile-phone reception is patchy, and it's very easy to get lost in bad weather. The Ordnance Survey's 1:25,000 Landranger maps are the best; they're incredibly detailed, showing practically every contour and natural feature. A compass is also very handy – assuming you know how to use it, of course.

Views

'No part of the country is more distinguished by its sublimity', mused the grand old bard of the Lakes, William Wordsworth, and a couple of centuries on, his words still ring true. The Lake District is justifiably famous across the UK (and the world) for its breathtaking landscapes, views and vistas.

Lakes

During the last ice age, huge ice sheets and glaciers etched out the Lake District's distinctive fells and valleys. When the ice retreated between 15,000 and 10,000 years ago, glacial meltwater became trapped, forming the lakes for which the Lake District is now famous.

Fells

Fell, the Cumbrian word for hill, comes from the Old Norse *fjell* – a legacy of the Vikings who once settled here to farm. While the rolling fields and green hills are picturesque, they're actually not natural: centuries of hill farming have removed most trees. Without its sheep, the Lake District's fells and valleys would quickly revert to scrub, heath and woodland.

Coast

Cumbria's coastline is worth exploring – a bleakly beautiful landscape of sandy bays, grassy headlands, salt marshes and seaside villages, stretching from Morecambe Bay to the shores of the Solway Coast.

Best Wild Valleys

Borrowdale & Buttermere Green and gorgeous, these side-by-side valleys are many people's favourites. (Buttermere pictured; p84)

Wasdale Wild and stark, overlooked by looming fells including Scafell Pike and Great Gable. (p117)

Great Langdale A hikers' favourite, with lots of fells to tackle. (p61)

Ennerdale A project to 'rewild' this remote valley is currently underway. (p117)

Haweswater Few people explore this eastern valley and its man-made reservoir. (p106)

JUSTIN FOULKES / LONELY PLANET ©

Best Beauty Spots

Tarn Hows A picture-perfect lake that's actually man-made. (p77)

Fell Foot Park This country park offers one of the best views of Windermere. (p48)

Watendlath Tarn Up in the hills above Borrowdale, with a landmark bridge en route. (p91)

Grasmere Lake & Rydal Water Admire the view that inspired Wordsworth every day. (p59)

St Bees Head Bring binoculars to spot the teeming birdlife at this coastal headland. (p116)

Best Waterfalls

Stock Ghyll Force An easy stroll up from Ambleside. (p38)

Aira Force One of the best-known falls in all the Lakes; come early to avoid crowds. (p98)

Dungeon Ghyll Climb up for a fine panorama over Great Langdale. (p57)

Lodore Falls An impressive cascade at the southern end of Derwentwater. (p92)

'A fine chasm': Scale Force

At 170ft, Scale Force is the highest waterfall in the Lake District. Described by Wordsworth as 'a fine chasm, with a lofty, though but slender, fall of water', it's a bit off the beaten track – you'll find it in the valley of Buttermere, on the path from Crummock Water to the summit of Red Pike.

Literary Locations

Children's Writers

The most famous children's writer linked with the Lake District is Beatrix Potter, who fell in love with the area on childhood holidays, and later swapped her gentrified Kensington lifestyle entirely for the life of a sheep breeder and hill farmer. Her tales brim with Lakeland scenery; fans will spot countless locations from her books, especially around Hill Top (p66).

Another children's author associated with the area is Arthur Ransome, author of *Swallows and Amazons* books, the majority of which are set in a fictionalised version of the Lake District.

The Romantics

Inspired by nature and landscape, the Romantic poets of the late 18th and early 19th century found a natural home in the Lake District. The best-known figures are Samuel Taylor Coleridge, Robert Southey and William Wordsworth, who was born in Cumbria (or Cumberland as it was then known) and found a lifetime of inspiration here. You can visit several of his homes, and his former school in Hawkshead.

Best Beatrix Potter Sights

Hill Top Beatrix's story-book cottage in the village of Near Sawrey; expect crowds. (p66)

Beatrix Potter Gallery Seasonal exhibitions of Beatrix's work in the former offices of her husband, solicitor William Heelis. (p76)

Armitt Museum This Keswick museum has a collection of Beatrix's botanical paintings. (p46)

Wray Castle The Potter family stayed here regularly when Beatrix was a child. (pictured; p37)

ALLAN BAXTER / GETTY IMAGES ©

Best Wordsworth Sights

Dove Cottage The creeper-clad house where Wordsworth first lived with his sister Dorothy and young family. (p53)

Rydal Mount This grand house near Grasmere was home to the Wordsworth family for 37 years. (p59)

Hawkshead Grammar School Look out for the desk where naughty Willie carved his name. (p76)

Gowbarrow Park Stroll amongst the daffodils where Wordsworth 'wandered lonely as a cloud'. (p98)

Wordsworth House Wordsworth was born at this Georgian house in Cockermouth. (p94)

Lakes Legend: Alfred Wainwright

The patron saint of Lakeland fell-walking, accountant-turned-author Alfred Wainwright (p87), was born in Blackburn, but had a lifelong love affair with the Lake District, and eventually moved here when he was appointed to the Borough Treasurer's department in Kendal in 1941.

You can see a reconstruction of Wainwright's office in Kendal Museum (p140), view a plaque dedicated to him in the village church in Buttermere and, of course, visit his last resting place near the top of Haystacks (p87).

Drinking & Nightlife

The Lake District's inns have been slaking people's thirst for centuries, and trying some locally brewed ale in a traditional village pub is a real highlight of a visit here.

Ale

Like much of England, Cumbria's tipple of choice is real ale – preferably served warm and pumped straight from the barrel. Most pubs have a range of local ales to try: Jennings (p94) in Cockermouth is one of the main local breweries, and also offers guided tours and tastings.

Spirits

Since 2014, the Lake District has been home to its very own spirit-maker, the Lakes Distillery (p93), which now produces gin, vodka and several fruit liqueurs, as well as its very own whisky. The distillery offers a range of tours.

Best Breweries

Jennings Cumbria's biggest brewer is in Cockermouth, with nattily-named beers like Sneck Lifter and Cocker Hoop. (p94)

Barngates Brewery In-house brewery at the Drunken Duck Inn. Try the Cracker, Tag Lag or Chester's Strong and Ugly. (p76)

Coniston Brewery Home of the original Bluebird Bitter (now available in a pale XB variety) as well as the rich, red Old Man Ale. (p71)

JUSTIN FOULKES / LONELY PLANET ©

Best Traditional Inns

Wasdale Head Inn A haven for walkers since the early 19th century. (pictured; p117)

Old Dungeon Ghyll Whitewashed, low-ceilinged and full of charm. (p62)

Mortal Man Knockout views over Windermere from the beer garden. (p39)

Black Bull Coniston pub that brews Bluebird Bitter. (p71)

Best Nightlife

Crafty Baa Tiny bar; huge range of craft beers. (p44)

Brewery Arts Centre Film, theatre and events in Kendal. (p143)

Brickyard Grungy gig venue in Carlisle. (p131)

Square Orange Keswick's most popular hangout (great pizza too). (p82)

Hell Below A great spot for craft beer in Carlisle. (p131)

Cafe-Bar 26 A sophisticated wine bar in Keswick. (p83)

Hawkshead Brewery

A local favourite, this well-known craft brewery has its own beer hall (p44) in Staveley, 3 miles east of Windermere. Some classic brews from its core range include Hawkshead Bitter, dark Brodie's Prime and fruity Red. Guided tours can be arranged in advance, and are well worth the time.

History

Several thousand years of human history are etched into the Lakeland hills, from the neolithic era through to the Industrial Revolution and on into the present day. There are numerous castles, churches, abbeys and stately homes to visit, and some great museums.

Ancient History

The earliest settlers in the Lake District were neolithic people, who built many stone circles and standing stones, such as Castlerigg Stone Circle, near Keswick. The area was later conquered by the Celts, then the Romans, and much later by the Vikings, who settled here and introduced hill farming.

Middle Ages

During the early medieval era, several important abbeys were founded in Cumbria, while Carlisle Castle was built as an important northern stronghold during a series of Anglo-Scottish conflicts. It was a notoriously lawless area, known as the 'Debatable Lands'; bands of marauders known as 'Border Reivers' regularly raided the area. To protect themselves, aristocratic families fortified their houses with 'pele' towers.

Industry & Tourism

The Industrial Revolution brought major change to northern England, and the Lake District was no exception. Quarrying and mining exploited the area's rich minerals, while many factories and mills were built. The railway reached the Lakes in 1847, attracting huge numbers of Victorian and Edwardian tourists, as well as rich industrialists who built themselves lavish country estates.

The National Park

After nearly a century of campaigning against industrial exploitation, the Lake District became one

ROGER COULAM / ALAMY STOCK PHOTO ©

of the UK's first four national parks in 1951. In 2017, it was named a Unesco World Heritage Site in recognition of its unique landscapes and hill-farming culture.

Historic Houses

Blackwell House One of England's finest Arts and Crafts houses. (p42)

Brantwood The lakeside home of Victorian art critic and philosopher John Ruskin. (p75)

Levens Hall Elizabethan manor built around a fortified *pele* tower. (pictured; p143)

Holker Hall Glorious stately home surrounded by acres of parkland. (p110)

Dalemain A Georgian wonder near the shores of Ullswater. (p104)

Castles

Carlisle Castle This imposing stronghold was built to guard the stormy Scottish border. (p132)

Sizergh Castle The feudal seat of the Strickland dynasty. (p143)

Muncaster Castle Look out for resident spooks at this sprawling coastal castle. (p118)

Lowther Castle Once one of Cumbria's grandest castles, now an evocative ruin. (p138)

Penrith Castle A ruined 14th-century castle on the outskirts of Penrith. (p138)

Museums

Tullie House Cumbria's best museum, encompassing several millennia of history. (p133)

Keswick Museum Quirky exhibits here include a mummified cat and musical stones. (p81)

Armitt Museum Provides a good overview of Lakeland history. (p46)

Museum of Lakeland Life & Industry Reconstructed scenes from days gone by. (p140)

Kendal Museum Stuffed beasties, archaeological artefacts and minerals galore. (p140)

Festivals & Events

The Lake District has a line-up of lively festivals and events throughout the year, ranging from traditional country fairs to walking festivals. As always, it pays to plan ahead, as accommodation can be hard to come by around the most popular times.

Big Festivals

The Lake District is the natural home of some of the UK's biggest mountain-sport festivals, including the **Keswick Mountain Festival** (www.keswickmountainfestival.co.uk; May) and the **Kendal Mountain Festival** (www.mountainfest.co.uk; November). Music-lovers shouldn't miss the **Kendal Calling** (p138), held on the Lowther Estate in July. Fans of fine beer and gourmet food should check out the **Keswick Beer Festival** (www.keswickbeerfestival.co.uk; June) and **Taste Cumbria** (www.tastecumbria.com; May) respectively.

Traditional Festivals

The Lake District is home to a wonderful array of local festivals. Traditionalists will love the **Cumberland County Show** (www.cumberlandshow.co.uk), which is Cumbria's largest agricultural show, and features Cumbrian wrestling, dressage displays, prize bulls and sheepdog displays. In a similar vein is the **Westmorland County Show** (www.westmorlandshow.co.uk), one of Britain's oldest agricultural shows. More bizarre is the **Egremont Crab Fair** (www.egremontcrabfair.com; mid-September), where competitors pull their ugliest expressions trying to win this historic gurning competition.

Sporting Events

Those who enjoy a physical challenge will find plenty to do in the Lake District. In June the waters of Windermere become a gigantic swimming pool during the **Great**

PENNY WATSON / ALAMY STOCK PHOTO ©

North Swim (www.greatrun.org/great-swim/great-north-swim). Cyclists love/hate the **Fred Whitton Challenge** (pictured; www.fredwhittonchallenge.org.uk), a 112-mile slog over the Lake District's six highest passes. While every August, hundreds of fell-runners tackle 6500 feet of ascent and 17 miles of fells during the **Borrowdale Fell Race** (www.borrowdalefellrunners.co.uk).

Best Local Festivals

Ambleside Rushbearing Processions of rushbearers parade through the streets in July. (p47)

Grasmere Sports Day Guides racing, Cumbrian wrestling and hound trailing at Grasmere's August sports day. (p55)

Dalemain Marmalade Festival Marmalade-making becomes an art form at this hotly-contested February festival. (p105)

World's Greatest Liar Competition Fibbers fight it out in an attempt to tell the biggest whopper – lawyers aren't allowed. (p117)

Country Shows

The Lake District's long history of hill farming makes its country shows an important part of the social calendar – many have been going for hundreds of years. The big ones of the year are the Cumberland and Westmorland County Shows, but there are many smaller fairs held throughout the year.

For Kids

ALISON THOMPSON / ALAMY STOCK PHOTO ©

The Lake District has scores of activities that are guaranteed to keep kids (big and little) entertained. They're especially handy in case of rainy days – which do happen in the Lakes from time to time, in case you haven't heard.

Best Activities

Honister Pass Delve the depths of an old slate mine, then try a via ferrata. (p93)

Grizedale Forest Charge through the forest on a network of bike trails. (p77)

Go Ape Clamber through the treetops on Whinlatter's high-wire assault course. There's another one in Grizedale. (p92)

Brockhole The Lake District's main visitor centre has adventure playgrounds and treetop nets to clamber. (p152)

Ravenglass & Eskdale Railway Ride this dinky railway, affectionately known as La'al Ratty. (pictured; p118)

World of Beatrix Potter Watch Benjamin Bunny and co come to life. (p42)

Best Museums

Lakeland Motor Museum A fine collection of antique automobiles, including a replica of Donald Campbell's famous *Bluebird* boat. (p49)

Derwent Pencil Museum See the world's biggest pencil. (p81)

Best Animal Encounters

Muncaster Castle Visit the hawk and owl centre. (p118)

Whinlatter Forest Watch for red squirrels at the forest visitor centre. (p92)

Lakes Aquarium Learn about what goes on at the bottom of the lakes. (p48)

The Home of Postman Pat

Kentmere Valley to the east of Windermere provided the model for John Cunliffe's classic BBC TV series, *Postman Pat*. Accompanied by his long-suffering cat, Jess, Pat's adventures have been a staple feature on British screens since the early 1980s.

Shopping

SIMON WHALEY / ALAMY STOCK PHOTO ©

Just because you're in the middle of a national park doesn't mean you can't indulge in a spot of retail therapy. Everyone should take a Lake District memento back with them – if only to munch on the long journey home.

Best Souvenirs

Wainwright guides The definitive walkers' guides are available in all good Lakeland bookshops, including the excellent Sam Read in Grasmere. (p55)

Grasmere gingerbread Produced to a secret recipe since 1854 at Sarah Nelson's Gingerbread Shop. (pictured; p55)

Kendal Mintcake Shops all around the Lakes sell this calorific bar, famously carried by Edmund Hillary and Tenzing Norgay en route to Everest.

A piece of slate You can buy authentic Lakeland slate from the shop at Honister Slate Mine. (p93)

Best Food Shops

Low Sizergh Barn Shelves stocked with Cumbrian goodies, from chutneys and cheeses to beers and raw milk! (p143)

Cartmel Village Shop The home of sticky toffee pudding. (p123)

Holker Food Hall Stock up on venison and saltmarsh lamb reared on the estate. (p110)

Stockghyll Fine Food A great deli in the middle of bustling Ambleside. (p47)

JJ Graham A lovely, old-fashioned grocer in Penrith. (p139)

Hawkshead Relish Company Jams and chutneys galore. (p77)

Four Perfect Days

Day 1

PAUL THOMPSON IMAGES / ALAMY STOCK PHOTO ©

Beginning in **Bowness-on-Windermere** (p42), drive south along Windermere's western shore, making pit-stops at the Arts-and-Crafts masterpiece of **Blackwell House** (p42) and **Fell Foot Park** (pictured; p48) for epic Windermere views. Continue round the lake to visit the **Lakeland Motor Museum** (p49) and take a trip on the quaint **Lakeside & Haverthwaite Railway** (p49). Drive up Windermere's east side to National Trust–owned **Wray Castle** (p37), where Beatrix Potter's family liked to holiday. Complete your Windermere circular in **Ambleside** (p46), followed by dinner at the **Old Stamp House** (p46) or **Lake Road Kitchen** (p46) in Ambleside.

Day 2

JOHN MORRISON / ALAMY STOCK PHOTO ©

From **Ambleside** (p46), head west to **Coniston Water** (p72) for a cruise on the **Steam Yacht Gondola** (p72) and a morning exploring John Ruskin's home, **Brantwood** (p75). Catch the boat back to Coniston and have lunch at the superb **Drunken Duck** (pictured; p76). Walk around the lake of **Tarn Hows** (p77), pop into **Hawkshead** (p76) for a visit to the **Beatrix Potter Gallery** (p76) and Wordsworth's alma mater, **Hawkshead Grammar School** (p76). Arrive at Beatrix Potter's cottage of **Hill Top** (p66) for one of the last tours of the day, then catch the **Windermere Ferry** (p148) back across the lake, followed by dinner at the **Mason's Arms** (p45) or **Brown Horse Inn** (p45).

Day 3

EDWARD HAYLAN / SHUTTERSTOCK ©

On day three, head north to the village of **Grasmere** (pictured; p52) to visit two of Wordsworth's homes, **Dove Cottage** (p53) and **Rydal Mount** (p59). Detour west past Elterwater to see the impressive valley of **Great Langdale** (p61); have lunch at the quaint **Old Dungeon Ghyll** (p62) or the nearby **Eltermere Inn** (p61). Backtrack to Grasmere, and then head north to the attractive town of **Keswick** (p80) for a cruise on the delightful lake of **Derwentwater** (p90). If there's enough time, you might just about fit in a sunset drive through the valleys of **Borrowdale** (p84) and **Buttermere** (p84), divided by the windswept **Honister Pass** (p85).

Day 4

DAVID STEELE / SHUTTERSTOCK ©

After overnighting in Keswick, head east towards Penrith, then turn south along the west side of **Ullswater** (p97). Follow the road south past **Gowbarrow Park** (p98) to the village of **Glenridding**. Cruise round the lake on one of the **Ullswater 'Steamers'** (pictured; p103), then continue south up and over the winding **Kirkstone Pass** (p107). Detour through **Troutbeck** (p39), stopping at the **Mortal Man** (p39) for a late lunch, then near Windermere, turn eastwards towards Kendal (it's worth popping into the **Hawkshead Brewery** (p44) at Staveley Yard if you have time). In Kendal, visit the **Abbot Hall Art Gallery** (p140) or **Sizergh Castle** (p143), and try the **Moon Highgate** (p142) or the **Wheatsheaf Inn** (p143) for dinner.

Need to Know

For detailed information, see Survival Guide (p145)

Currency
Pound (£)

Language
English

Visas
Generally not needed for stays of up to six months.

Money
ATMs widely available; credit cards widely accepted.

Time
Cumbria is on GMT/UTC.

Phones
The UK uses the GSM 900/1800 mobile network. Signal can be patchy outside main towns. Check roaming charges: EU residents can use home rates, but rates for other overseas travellers can be high.

Daily Budget

Budget: Less than £60

Dorm beds: £15–30

Cheap meals in cafes and pubs: £7–11

Local buses £5-10

Midrange: £60–130

Double room in a midrange hotel or B&B: £65–130

Main course in a midrange restaurant: £10–20

Lakes Day Ranger travel pass: £23

Top End: More than £130

Four-star hotel room: from £130 (London from £200)

Three-course meal in a good restaurant: around £40

Car rental per day: from £35

Useful Websites

Lake District National Park Authority (www.lakedistrict.gov.uk) The official site for the national park.

Visit Cumbria (www.visitcumbria.com) The main tourist portal for sights and activities across Cumbria, including the Lake District.

National Trust (www.nationaltrust.co.uk) Useful for information on NT-owned sights such as Hill Top.

Arriving in The Lake District

Most people drive to the Lake District, but it's also possible to arrive by train, coach and air.

Carlisle Train Station

Carlisle is on the main West Coast train line from London Euston to Manchester and Glasgow.

Windermere Train Station

The closest train station to the Lake District is Oxenholme, which is also on the main West Coast Line. From Oxenholme, local trains run directly to Kendal and Windermere Town.

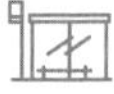

Getting Around

The vast majority of travellers explore by car - but a good bus network means you don't necessarily need your own wheels.

Bicycle

Cycling is a fun way to explore, but be prepared for hills. Some buses have space for carrying bikes.

Boat

There are boat cruises on Windermere, Coniston Water, Ullswater and Derwentwater. Windermere also has a cross-lake ferry for bikes, passengers and cars.

Bus

Most towns and villages are served by bus, although services are reduced in winter. Stagecoach (www.stagecoachbus.com) is the main operator: you can download timetables and see fares on its website.

Car

Having a car gives you maximum freedom. Downsides include heavy traffic (especially around holidays), expensive parking and a shortage of petrol stations outside main towns.

Lake District Regions

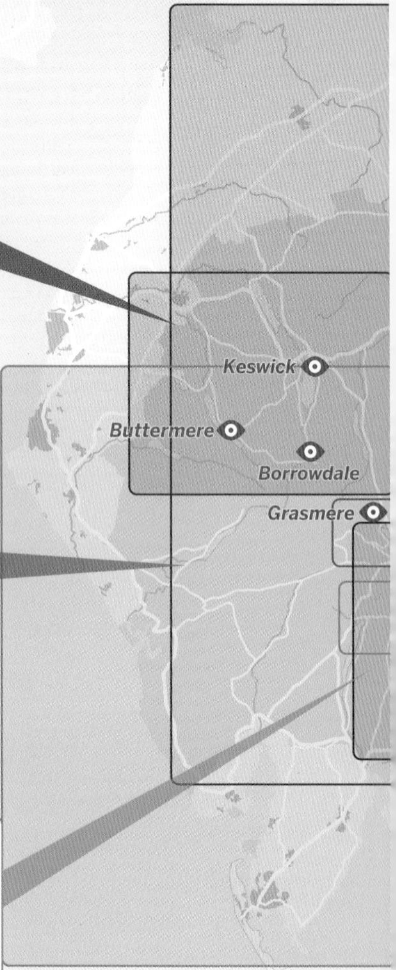

Keswick & Derwentwater (p79)

Keswick is a busy market town nestled beside the island-studded lake of Derwentwater, and a useful base for exploring Borrowdale, Buttermere and Whinlatter Forest.

Grasmere & Central Lake District (p51)

This lakeside village is best known as the former home of William Wordsworth, but it's also a gateway to the dramatic, fell-framed valley of Great Langdale.

Hill Top, Coniston & Hawkshead (p65)

Guarded by the hulking Old Man of Coniston, Coniston Water inspired the classic children's story *Swallows and Amazons*, while nearby Hawkshead has Beatrix Potter connections.

Keswick
Buttermere
Borrowdale
Grasmere

Inland Cumbria (p127)

Visit the sturdy market towns of Penrith and Kendal, admire the topiary of Levens Hall and gaze over the Scottish border from the battlements of Carlisle Castle.

Gowbarrow Park & Aira Force

Ullswater (p97)

Cruise the stately lake aboard one of Ullswater's historic 'steamers', then tackle the surrounding fells, including the knife-edge ridge to the top of Helvellyn.

Windermere

Hill Top

Windermere & Around (p35)

Cruise the islands and wander the shorelines of England's largest lake, the centre of Lakeland tourism for more than a century.

Western Lakes & Cumbrian Coast (p109)

Often overlooked by visitors, Cumbria's wind-blown coastline offers sandy beaches, historic ports, stately homes and dramatic headlands.

GIVE
ENDS

Explore The Lake District

The Lake District Walking Tours

The Lake District Driving Tour

Grasmere (p52) ANDREW ROLAND / SHUTTERSTOCK ©

Explore

Windermere & Around

Stretching for 10.5 miles between Ambleside and Newby Bridge, Windermere is the largest body of water anywhere in England. The western shore is home to the busy towns of Bowness-on-Windermere and Ambleside, while the east side is much less developed.

Start your day with a wander round the shops and jetties of Bowness-of-Windermere, then enjoy a cruise (p37) around the lake and its islands, with an optional excursion to either Fell Foot Park (p48) or Wray Castle (p37). Alight at Ambleside for lunch – a good budget option is the Great North Pie (p47) or go gourmet at the Old Stamp House (p46). After lunch, visit the Armitt Museum (p46) and walk to Stock Ghyll Force (p39). Bus back to Windermere, and book dinner at one of the local gastropubs – the Mason's Arms (p45) and Brown Horse Inn (p45) are both reliably good.

Getting There & Around

The Windermere Ferry (p148) shuttles between the lake's east and west sides.

The 555/556 Lakeslink and open-top 599 run to Ambleside, Grasmere and Keswick. The 505 travels from Bowness to Coniston via Ambleside and Hawkshead.

The A591 links Windermere Town and Ambleside. The A592 tracks Windermere's eastern shore from Bowness-on-Windermere to the lake's southern end.

Windermere is on the branch line to Kendal and Oxenholme, with connections to Edinburgh, Manchester and London Piccadilly.

Windermere & Around Map on p40

Windermere (p36)

Top Sights

Windermere & the Islands

Windermere gets its name from the old Norse, Vinandr mere (Vinandr's lake; so Lake Windermere is actually tautologous). Encompassing 5.7 sq miles between Ambleside and Newby Bridge, the lake is a mile wide at its broadest point, with a maximum depth of about 220m. It's a lovely place to take a cruise or hire a boat for the afternoon, but it is far and away the busiest of the lakes.

MAP P40, C3

Windermere's Islands

The largest of Windermere's 18 islands is **Belle Isle** (pictured), covering 16 hectares and an 18th-century Italianate mansion, while the smallest is **Maiden Holme**. The lake's shoreline is owned by a mix of private landowners, the National Park Authority and the National Trust, but the lake itself belongs to the people of Windermere.

Out on the Lake

Cruising has been an essential part of every Windermere itinerary since the 19th century. **Windermere Lake Cruises** (☎015394-43360; www.windermere-lakecruises.co.uk) explores different areas of the lake.

It's also possible to explore the lake under your own steam; from April to October, rowing boats (£16 per hour) and cute cabin motor boats (from £30 for two adults per hour; children under 16 free) can be hired beside the Bowness piers.

Alternatively, **Low Water Watersports** (☎015394-39441; www.englishlakes.co.uk/low-wood-bay/watersports; Low Bay Marina), halfway between Ambleside and Windermere, offers waterskiing, sailing and kayaking and has rowing boats and motor boats for hire. Kayaks cost from £15 per hour, canoes from £18 per hour.

There's a 10mph speed limit on the lake.

Wray Castle

An impressive sight with its turrets and battlements, this mock-Gothic **castle** (NT; www.nationaltrust.org.uk/wray-castle; adult/child £9.60/4.80; ⏲10am-5pm) was built in 1840 for James Dawson, a retired doctor from Liverpool, but has been owned by the National Trust since 1929. Though the interior is largely empty, the lakeside grounds are glorious. It was once used as a holiday home by Beatrix Potter's family. The best way to arrive is by boat from Bowness, as there's limited parking.

★ Top Tips

Windermere Lake Cruises offers a number of ticket options:

- The **Freedom of the Lake** ticket (adult/child/family £20.80/10.40/56.50) allows a day's unlimited travel on all routes.
- The most popular route is the 45-minute **Islands Cruise** (adult/child/family £8.60/4.30/23), but several longer cruises are also available.
- The **Walkers' Ticket** allows you to cruise to Wray Castle, walk along the lake's western shore through Claife Heights to Ferry House, then catch a boat back to either Bowness, Brockhole or Ambleside.

✕ Take a Break

There are plenty of cafes in Bowness and Windermere Town, as well as tearooms at Wray Castle.

Walking Tour

Stock Ghyll Force & Wansfell Pike

This moderate hike from Ambleside takes in the summit of Wansfell Pike (1588ft), which offers a grand outlook over Windermere despite its relatively low profile. If you wish, you can just follow it as far as the waterfall of Stock Ghyll Force – but it's worth taking the time to do the full hike if you can. As always, good boots and a rainproof jacket are essential.

Walk Facts

Start Ambleside; 555 or 599 from Windermere or the 505 from Coniston

End Ambleside

Length 6 miles; four hours

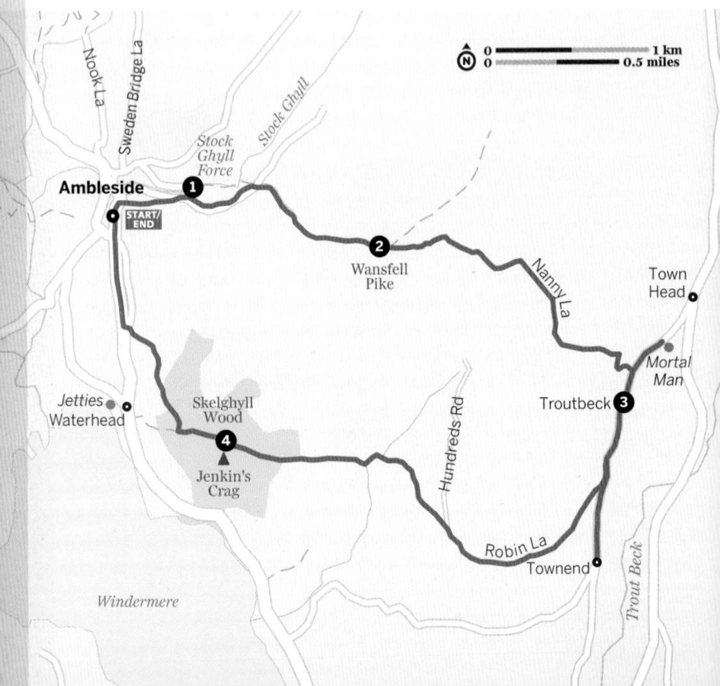

❶ Stock Ghyll Force

The trail starts on Stock Ghyll Lane behind the Market Hall. Follow the path up through the woods, following signs to **Stock Ghyll Force**, the 18m-high waterfall that clatters down the hillside right into the centre of Ambleside. It's a famous photo spot, so remember to carry your camera.

❷ Wansfell Pike

After viewing the falls, take the path leading to the right through a cast-iron Victorian turnstile. Turn left and follow the paved lane, then take the right-hand path leading sharply up the fellside (signed to Wansfell Pike). It's steep and can be slippery in places, although a stone staircase has been constructed at the worst bits.

You should reach the summit after around half an hour of climbing. The 'Pike' is actually one of two separate summits on Wansfell; **Baystones** (1601ft) to the northeast is higher, but **Wansfell Pike** is considered the superior summit thanks to its impressive outlook over Windermere and the distant Langdale range.

❸ Troutbeck

From the fell-top, follow the path east across the fells. After 20 minutes or so, the path joins up with a rough stone track known as Nanny Lane, which meanders steeply downhill into the pretty hamlet of **Troutbeck**, which is nestled among the fells to the north of Windermere, surrounded by green fields and drystone walls, with wonderful views over Windermere.

Troutbeck's oldest pub, the **Mortal Man** (☎015394-33193; www.themortalman.co.uk; mains £12.50-18.95) makes an excellent place for a pint stop, with its cracking fell-view beer garden. (If you're wondering about the curious name, have a look at the pub sign on your way in – it's taken from an old Lakeland rhyme.) Or, head down through the village for a visit to the medieval farmhouse of **Townend** (NT; ☎01539-432628; www.nationaltrust.org.uk/townend; adult/child £6.50/3.25; ⏲1-5pm Wed-Sun Mar-Oct, daily school holidays) and its collection of vintage farming ephemera.

❹ Skelghyll Wood

Just past the post office, take the rough track signposted as Robin Lane. Stay on the main track and follow the signs; after a while you'll pass High Skelghyll Farm and drop downhill into the National Trust–owned **Skelghyll Wood**. About halfway through the wood, a side-track leads to the famous outlook of **Jenkin's Crag** – try to time your arrival for late afternoon, when the sinking sun lights up Windermere and the Langdale Pikes.

Return to the main path and follow the track through the woods to Ambleside, emerging near the Waterhead jetties.

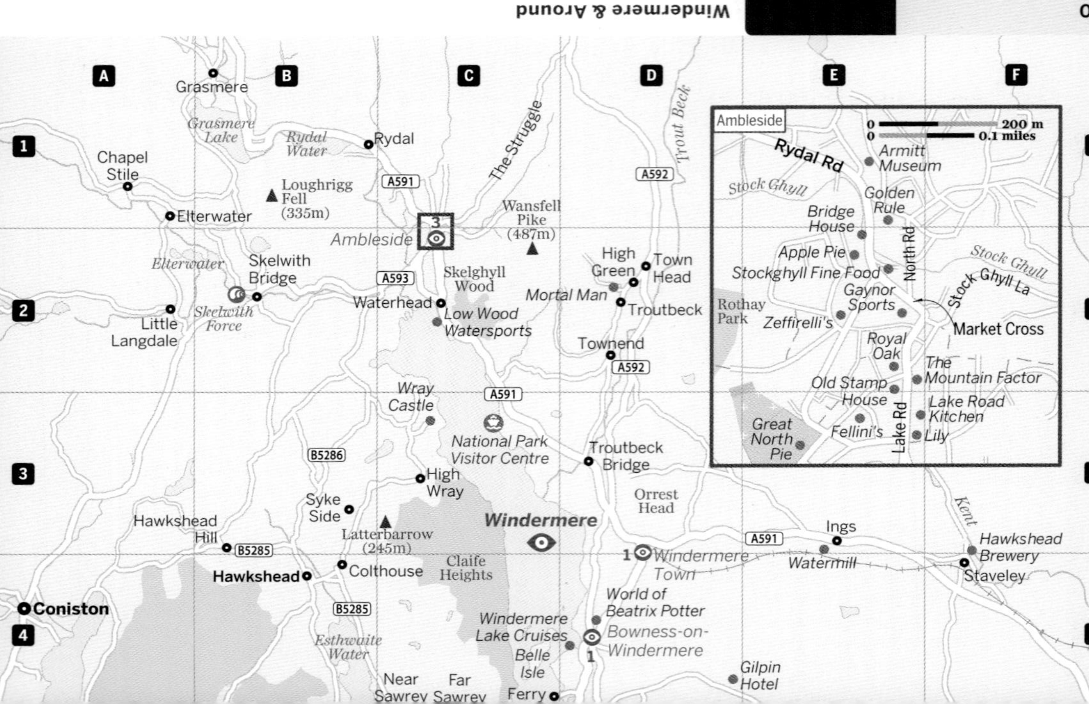
A
B
C
D
E
F
1
2
3
4
Grasmere
Grasmere Lake
Rydal Water
Rydal
The Struggle
Trout Beck
A592
Chapel Stile
Loughrigg Fell (335m)
A591
Wansfell Pike (487m)
Elterwater
3
Ambleside
Elterwater
Skelwith Bridge
A593
Skelghyll Wood
High Green
Town Head
Mortal Man
Troutbeck
Waterhead
Low Wood Watersports
Little Langdale
Skelwith Force
Townend
A592
Wray Castle
A591
National Park Visitor Centre
Troutbeck Bridge
B5286
High Wray
Orrest Head
Syke Side
Hawkshead Hill
Latterbarrow (245m)
Windermere
B5285
Hawkshead
Colthouse
Claife Heights
1
Windermere Town
A591
Ings
Watermill
Hawkshead Brewery
Staveley
Kent
Coniston
B5285
World of Beatrix Potter
Windermere Lake Cruises
Bowness-on-Windermere
1
Esthwaite Water
Belle Isle
Near Sawrey
Far Sawrey
Ferry
Gilpin Hotel
Ambleside
0
200 m
0
0.1 miles
Rydal Rd
Armitt Museum
Stock Ghyll
Golden Rule
Bridge House
Apple Pie
North Rd
Stock Ghyll
Stock Ghyll La
Stockghyll Fine Food
Gaynor Sports
Rothay Park
Zeffirelli's
Market Cross
Royal Oak
The Mountain Factor
Old Stamp House
Lake Road Kitchen
Great North Pie
Fellini's
Lake Rd
Lily

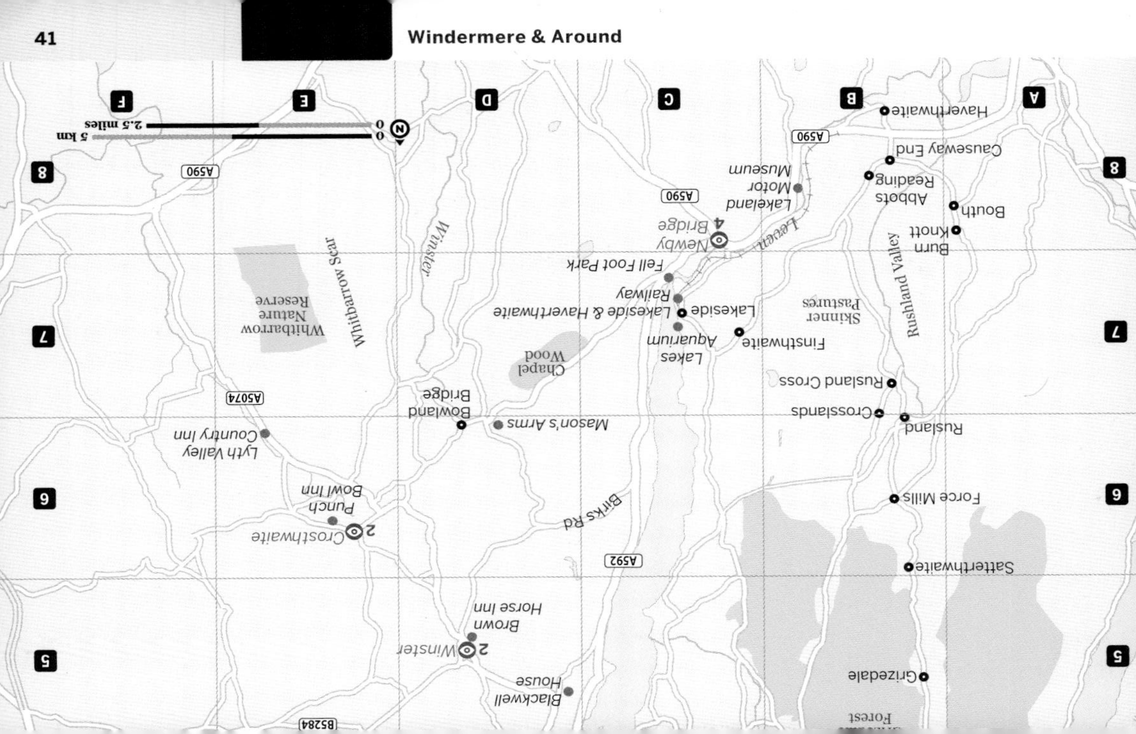

A
B
C
D
E
F
5
6
7
8
0
0
2.5 miles
5 km
Grizedale
Forest
Satterthwaite
Force Mills
Rusland
Crosslands
Rusland Cross
Rushland Valley
Burn Knott
Bouth
Abbots Reading
Causeway End
Haverthwaite
Skinner Pastures
Finsthwaite
Lakeside
Lakes Aquarium
Lakeside & Haverthwaite Railway
Fell Foot Park
4 Newby Bridge
Leven
Lakeland Motor Museum
A590
A592
Birks Rd
Mason's Arms
Chapel Wood
Bowland Bridge
Winster
Whitbarrow Scar
Whitbarrow Nature Reserve
A5074
Lyth Valley Country Inn
2 Crosthwaite
Punch Bowl Inn
2 Winster
Brown Horse Inn
Blackwell House
B5284

Windermere Town & Bowness-on-Windermere

1 MAP P40, D4

Confusingly, the town of Windermere is split in two: Windermere Town is actually 1.5 miles from the lake, at the top of a steep hill, while Bowness-on-Windermere (usually shortened just to Bowness) sits on the lake's eastern shore.

The **World of Beatrix Potter** (015394-88444; www.hop-skip-jump.com; Crag Brow, Bowness-on-Windermere; adult/child/family £7.95/3.95/22, incl theatre show £17/10/50; 10am-5.30pm Apr-Sep, to 4.30pm Oct-Mar) themed attraction brings to life various scenes from Beatrix Potter's books, including Peter Rabbit's garden, Mr McGregor's greenhouse, Mrs Tiggy-winkle's kitchen and Jemima Puddle-Duck's glade (there's even a themed tearoom). A recent addition is the *Where is Peter Rabbit?* musical theatre show (adult/child/family £10.50/8/35, late May to September), which features puppets and characters from the stories. It's squarely aimed at kids, but adult Potter fans might enjoy indulging their inner child.

Two miles south of Bowness on the B5360, **Blackwell House** (015394-46139; www.blackwell.org.uk; adult/child under 16yr £8/free; 10.30am-5pm Apr-Oct, to 4pm Feb, Mar, Nov & Dec) is a glorious example of the 19th-century Arts and Crafts Movement, which championed handmade goods and quality over the mass-produced mentality of the Industrial Revolution. Designed by Mackay Hugh

Brockhole National Park Visitor Centre

If you're a first-timer to the Lakes, the national park's main visitor centre at **Brockhole** (015394-46601; www.brockhole.co.uk; 10am-5pm) should definitely be your first port of call. It's housed in a fine mansion built in 1895 for the Mancunian silk merchant William Henry Aldolphus Gaddum, but has served as a visitor centre since 1969. There are informative displays on the geology, environment and history of the national park, as well as a kids' playground and lakeside gardens designed by Thomas Mawson, who also planned the grounds at Blackwell House. Staff can help plan sights and activities and also run regular guided walks and talks; check the website for the latest events.

The visitor centre is 3 miles from Windermere on the A591. Windermere Lake Cruises and buses 555 and 599 all make stops at Brockhole.

Dining room, Blackwell House

Baillie Scott for Sir Edward Holt, a wealthy brewer, the house shimmers with Arts and Crafts details: light, airy rooms, bespoke craftwork, wood panelling, stained glass and delft tiles. The mock-medieval Great Hall and serene White Drawing Room are particularly fine.

Windermere and Bowness both have plenty of options when it comes time for a break.

The definition of a neighbourhood bistro, **Francine's** (015394-44088; www.francinesrestaurant windermere.co.uk; 27 Main Rd, Windermere Town; 2-/3-course dinner menu £16.95/19.95; 10am-2.30pm & 6.30-11pm Tue-Sat) is a locals' favourite and if you visit more than once you'll probably be greeted by name. It's a tiny space with crammed-in tables, so watch your elbows with your neighbours. Food is solid if not stellar, with tastes tending toward the hearty, such as roast guinea fowl, confit pork belly and chicken supreme.

Seafood might not be something you immediately think of when deciding what to eat in Windermere, but Paul White's first-class fish restaurant **Hooked** (015394-48443; www.hooked windermere.co.uk; Ellerthwaite Sq, Windermere Town; mains £19.95-21.95; 5.30-10.30pm Tue-Sun) is well worth considering. He likes to keep things classic: hake with Mediterranean veg and pesto, sea trout with peas and pancetta, or lemon sole with capers and parsley butter. It's small, so bookings are essential.

Gilpin House

Windermere's B&Bs might be pushing up their rates to silly levels, but the famously posh country-house retreat of **Gilpin House** (☎015394-88818; www.gilpinlodge.co.uk; Crook Rd; r £275-465; P) shows them how it should be done. The fabulously fancy rooms are named after fells, garden suites have their own decks and outdoor hot tubs, and the exclusive Lake House nearby comes with its own chauffeur.

A superb Michelin-starred restaurant, a lovely spa and hectares of grounds complete the high-class package.

Windermere gets its own boutique coffee house in **Homeground** (☎015394-44863; www.homegroundcafe.co.uk; 56 Main Rd, Windermere Town; coffee £2-4, mains £7-10; ⏰9am-5pm), serving excellent flat whites, pourovers and ristrettos, accompanied by a fine display of milk art. It's super for brunch too. All in all, a thoroughly welcome new addition to town.

The craft-beer revolution comes to Windermere at **Crafty Baa** (☎015394-88002; 21 Victoria St, Windermere Town; ⏰11am-11pm), with a vast selection of brews: Czech pilsners, weissbiers, smoked lagers, even mango, gooseberry and coconut beers, chalked up on a wall of slates and served (if you wish) with snack platters. The space (a former house) is tiny, but plans are afoot to expand next door.

Bowness' oldest boozer, **Hole in T'Wall** (☎015394-43488; Fallbarrow Rd, Bowness-on-Windermere; ⏰11am-11pm) dates back to 1612 and offers lashings of rough-beamed, low-ceilinged atmosphere.

Winster, Crosthwaite & Around

2 ◉ MAP P40, D5, E6

Two miles from Windermere in Ings, resolutely traditional **Watermill** (☎01539-821309; www.watermillinn.co.uk; Ings; mains £11-20; ⏰11am-11pm Mon-Sat, to 10.30pm Sun) is exactly what you'd expect from a Cumbrian pub – beamed ceilings, whitewashed walls, log fires, hand pumps and all. Throw in old-fashioned pub grub and a wide choice of ales, including home-brewed Collie Wobbles, and it's no wonder it's scooped lots of local awards.

East of Ings, in Staveley, the renowned craft brewery **Hawkshead Brewery** (☎01539-822644; www.hawksheadbrewery.co.uk; Mill Yard, Staveley) has its own beer hall. Core beers include Hawkshead Bitter, dark Brodie's Prime and fruity Red. Guided tours can be arranged in advance.

Three miles southeast from Windermere in Winster, the **Brown Horse Inn** (015394-43443; www.thebrownhorseinn.co.uk; Winster; mains £12.95-16.95; lunch noon-2pm, dinner 6-9pm) is a popular dining pub. Produce is sourced from the Brown Horse Estate, furnishing the chefs with meat and game such as venison, spring lamb and pigeon. Beams and fireplaces conjure a rustic atmosphere, and there are several ales on tap from the in-house Winster Brewery.

A touch further south in Crosthwaite, **Punch Bowl Inn** (015395-68237; www.the-punch-bowl.co.uk; Crosthwaite; mains £15.95-24.50; noon-4pm & 5.30-8.30pm; P) is a renowned gastropub that has long been known for its top-notch food. Whitewashed outside, carefully modernised inside, it's a cosy, inviting space to dine. Chef Scott Fairweather's superb food blends classic dishes with cheffy ingredients (oyster mousse, potato croquettes, pea fricassée, salsify).

Three miles east of Crosthwaite, near Bowlands Bridge, the marvellous **Mason's Arms** (015395-68486; www.masonsarmsstrawberrybank.co.uk; Winster; mains £12.95-18.95) is a local secret. The rafters, flagstones and cast-iron range haven't changed in centuries, and the patio has to-die-for views across fields and fells. The food is hearty – Cumbrian stewpot, slow-roasted Cartmel lamb – and there are lovely rooms and cottages for rent (£175 to £350). In short, a cracker.

Stock Ghyll Force (p39)

Ambleside

3 MAP P40, C2

Ringed by fells, Ambleside is a favourite base for hikers, with a cluster of outdoors shops and plenty of cosy pubs and cafes providing fuel for adventures.

Despite some damage incurred during the 2015 floods, Ambleside's excellent little **Armitt Museum** (015394-31212; www.armitt.com; Rydal Rd; adult/child £5/free; 10am-5pm) is now back up and running.

It hosts some intriguing seasonal exhibitions alongside its core collection, populated with artefacts relating to important Lakeland characters such as National Trust founder Canon Hardwicke Rawnsley, pioneering Lakeland photographers Herbert Bell and the Abraham Brothers, and a certain Beatrix Potter, who bequeathed a number of botanical watercolours to the museum, along with several 1st editions of her books.

Bridge House

Ambleside's best-known landmark, this tiny cottage spans the clattering brook of Stock Ghyll. Now occupied by a National Trust shop, it's thought to have originally been built as an apple store.

The village abounds with options for a meal, from fine dining to perfect pies.

In the cellar of the building where Wordsworth worked as distributor of stamps, fine-dining bistro **Old Stamp House** (015394-32775; www.oldstamphouse.com; Church St; dinner mains £24-28; 12.30-2pm Wed-Sat, 6.30-10pm Tue-Sat) champions Cumbrian produce, much of it raised, caught, shot or cured within a few miles' radius. You'll find ingredients like Arctic char, Herdwick hogget and roe deer on the menu, partnered with foraged ingredients, surprising flavour combinations and delicate sauces, all impeccably presented. Outstanding.

Much-lauded new bistro **Lake Road Kitchen** (015394-22012; www.lakeroadkitchen.co.uk; Lake Rd; 5-/8-course tasting menu £65/90; 6-9.30pm Wed-Sun) has brought some dazzle to Ambleside's dining scene. Its Noma-trained head chef, James Cross,explores the 'food of the north', and his multicourse tasting menus are chock-full of locally sourced, seasonal and foraged ingredients, from shore-sourced seaweed to forest-picked mushrooms. Presentation is impeccable, flavours are experimental and the Scandi-inspired decor is just so.

For a quick lunch stop, you won't go far wrong at **Apple Pie** (015394-33679; www.applepieambleside.co.uk; Rydal Rd; lunches £4-10; 9am-5.30pm), a friendly little cafe, which serves stuffed

Ambleside Rushbearing

Ambleside's oldest festival is the annual rushbearing ceremony, which sees local parishioners parading around the town's streets carrying big bundles of rushes, reeds and grasses, carried in sheafs or arranged into ornamental shapes. The tradition dates back to the days when local churches had mud rather than slate floors, and rushes were laid underfoot to keep the church interior dry (and also to mask any smells from the graveyard next door).

The ceremony is usually held on the first Saturday in July. Nearby Grasmere holds its rushbearing ceremony on the third Saturday in July.

sandwiches, hot pies, baked spuds and yummy cakes (the apple pie is a local legend). Everything is available to either eat in or take away.

Based in Wilmslow, much-garlanded pie maker **Great North Pie** (01625 522112; www.greatnorthpie.co; Unit 2, The Courtyard, Rothay Rd; pies £4-8; 9am-5pm) has opened an Ambleside outlet, and it's rightly become a town favourite. Go for a classic such as Swaledale beef mince or Lancashire cheese and onion, or opt for something on the seasonal pie menu: they're all delicious.

A beloved local landmark, **Zeffirelli's** (015394-33845; www.zeffirellis.com; Compston Rd; pizzas & mains £8-15; 11am-10pm) is often packed out for its quality pizza and pasta. The £21.75 Double Feature deal includes two courses and a ticket to the cinema next door.

Vegetarians won't go hungry thanks to the sophisticated 'vegeterranean' food at **Fellini's** (015394-32487; www.fellinisambleside.com; Church St; mains £12-15; 5.30-10pm;). The dishes are creative and beautifully presented – think delicate Moroccan filo parcels, stuffed portobello mushrooms and radicchio provolne ravioli.

For premium Cumbrian cheeses, chutneys, cold cuts, beers and breadsticks, **Stockghyll Fine Food** (015394-31865; www.stockghyllfinefood.co.uk; Rydal Rd; sandwiches £3-4; 9am-5pm Wed-Sun) is impossible to top in Ambleside.

You won't be short on options for a drink in Ambleside either.

Right in the heart of town, the old whitewashed **Royal Oak** (015394-33382; www.greeneking-pubs.co.uk; Market Pl) is the best pub in Ambleside, with hearty pub mains, good ales and a busy outside terrace. It's a hikers' favourite.

Ambleside's **Golden Rule** (015394-32257; www.robinsonsbrewery.com/goldenrule; Smithy Brow) is a traditional pub with plenty of local ales on tap, mostly from the owners' Robinson's Brewery.

For something a little more upscale than Ambleside's trad pubs, head down to slinky wine bar **Lily** (☎015394-33175; www.thelilybar.co.uk; 12-14 Lake Rd; ⏲noon-11pm) for a glass of wine and a spot of local music. There are candlelit tables and armchairs to sink into – and 'speedquizzing' on Wednesday nights.

Around Newby Bridge

4 ◉ MAP P40, C8

At the southern end of the lake near Newby Bridge, **Lakes Aquarium** (☎015395-30153; www.lakesaquarium.co.uk; Lakeside; adult/child £7.45/5.45; ⏲10am-6pm) explores a range of underwater habitats from tropical Africa through to Morecambe Bay. Windermere Lake Cruises (p37) and the Lakeside & Haverthwaite Railway (p49) stop right beside the aquarium, or you could catch bus 6/X6 from Bowness. There's a £1 discount per ticket for online bookings.

Nearby, the 7-hectare lakeside estate of **Fell Foot Park** (NT; www.nationaltrust.org.uk/fell-foot-park; free; ⏲8am-8pm Apr-Sep, 9am-5pm Oct-Mar, cafe 10am-5pm) belonged to a manor house. It's now owned by the National Trust, and its shoreline paths and grassy lawns are ideal for picnics. There's a small cafe and rowing boats are available for hire.

Built to carry ore and timber to the ports at Ulverston and Barrow,

Mason's Arms (p45)

ROB COUSINS / ALAMY STOCK PHOTO ©

Lyth & Winster Valleys

To the east of Fell Foot Park, a twisting road (signed towards Kendal) leads northeast into the little-explored Lyth and Winster Valleys. They feel wonderfully remote, even though they're only a short drive from Windermere – a quality which no doubt appealed to Arthur Ransome, who lived nearby at Low Ludderburn while penning *Swallows and Amazons*.

Lyth and Winster are known for their crops of Westmorland damsons, a soft fruit related to the plum, used to flavour everything from jam and juices to chocolate and gin. In late summer you'll often see stalls by the side of the road selling damson-flavoured goodies.

There are some great local options for dinner too – try the Mason's Arms (p45), the Punch Bowl Inn (p45) or the **Lyth Valley Country Inn** (Map p40; ☎015395-68295; www.lythvalley.com; Lyth; mains £14-23; P 📶).

the vintage steam trains of **Lakeside & Haverthwaite Railway** (☎015395-31594; www.lakesiderailway.co.uk; adult/child/family return from Haverthwaite to Lakeside £6.90/3.45/19, 1-day rover ticket adult/child £10/5; ⏲mid-Mar–Oct) puff their way between Haverthwaite, near Ulverston, and Newby Bridge and Lakeside. There are five to seven trains a day, timed to correspond with the Windermere cruise boats; you can buy combo tickets that include an onward lake cruise to Bowness or Ambleside.

Two miles south of Newby Bridge on the A590, **Lakeland Motor Museum** (☎015395-30400; www.lakelandmotormuseum.co.uk; Backbarrow; adult/child £8.75/5.25; ⏲9.30am-5.30pm Apr-Sep, to 4.30pm Oct-Mar) houses a wonderful collection of antique cars: classic (Minis, Austin Healeys, MGs), sporty (DeLoreans, Audi Quattros, Aston Martins) and downright odd (Scootacars, Amphicars). There are also quirky exhibits on the history of caravans and vintage bicycles. A separate building explores Donald and Malcolm Campbell's record attempts on Coniston Water, with replicas of the 1935 Bluebird car and 1967 *Bluebird K7* boat. Online bookings get a 10% discount.

DOVE COTTAGE

Explore

Grasmere & Central Lake District

Grasmere acts as a geographical junction between the east and west of the Lake District, sandwiched between the rumpled peaks of Great Langdale and the gentle hummocks and open dales of the eastern fells. The village is best known as the former home of William Wordsworth.

It makes sense to start your visit at Dove Cottage (p53), Wordsworth's home from 1799 to 1808; the excellent Wordsworth Museum is next door. Explore the village, pay your respects at the poet's grave at St Oswald's Church (p53) and stop for gingerbread at Sarah Nelson's famous shop (p55). Have lunch at Brew (p54), then devote the afternoon to Rydal Mount (p59), another former Wordsworth home. Late afternoon, drive out to the rugged valley of Great Langdale (p61), before returning for dinner at the Eltermere Inn (p61) or Jumble Room (p54).

Getting There & Around

Bus 555 runs from Windermere to Grasmere via Ambleside, Rydal Church and Dove Cottage, then on to Keswick. The open-top bus 599 runs from Grasmere via Ambleside, Troutbeck Bridge, Windermere and Bowness. Bus 516 travels to Great Langdale, stopping at Ambleside, Skelwith Bridge, Elterwater and the Old Dungeon Ghyll hotel in Great Langdale.

The A591 links Ambleside to Grasmere. The A593 travels west from Ambleside to Great Langdale.

Central Lake District Map on p58

Dove Cottage (p53) VAL CORBETT / GETTYIMAGES ©

Top Sights

Grasmere

Huddled at the edge of an island-studded lake surrounded by woods, pastures and slate-coloured hills, Wordsworth's beloved village is a must-see. Several of the poet's former houses can be visited, as well as an excellent museum – and, poignantly, his family's plot in the village churchyard.

MAP P58, D2

www.lakedistrict.gov.uk/visiting/placestogo/aroundgrasmere

Village Sights

The tiny, creeper-clad **Dove Cottage** (015394-35544; www.wordsworth.org.uk; adult/child £8.95/free; 9.30am-5.30pm Mar-Oct, 10am-4.30pm Nov, Dec & Feb) – formerly a pub called the Dove & Olive Bough – was inhabited by William Wordsworth between 1799 and 1808. Wordsworth lived here with his sister Dorothy, wife Mary and three children, John, Dora and Thomas, until 1808 when the family moved to a nearby house at Allen Bank. The cottage's cramped rooms are full of artefacts – look out for the poet's passport, spectacles and a portrait (given to him by Sir Walter Scott) of his favourite dog, Pepper. Entry is by timed ticket to avoid overcrowding and includes an informative guided tour.

Dove Cottage tickets also include admission to the **Wordsworth Museum & Art Gallery** next door, which houses one of the nation's main collections relating to the Romantic movement. The Old Coffin Trail (p59) leads to another nearby Wordsworth home, Rydal Mount (p59).

Named after a Viking saint, Grasmere's medieval chapel **St Oswald's Church** (pictured; Church Stile) is where Wordsworth and his family attended church service every Sunday for many years. It's also their final resting place – the Wordsworth's family graves are tucked into a quiet corner of the churchyard under the spreading bows of a great yew tree. Inside the church you'll find Wordsworth's own prayer book and his favourite pew, marked by a plaque.

Eating

As traditionally English as a Sunday roast, the old-school **Baldry's Tea Room** (015394-35301; Red Lion Sq; lunch £5-9; 10am-5pm) is the spot for a classic cream tea served in a bone-china pot and accompanied by buttery scones, flapjacks or a slice of Victoria sponge. There are rarebits

★ Top Tips

- Grasmere gets very busy in summer, and the village car parks can often be full, so consider visiting by bus from Ambleside or Windermere.
- Guided visits to Dove Cottage run to specific timeslots; it's worth booking online in advance.

Take a Break

Grasmere has lots of lovely cafes that make a perfect sightseeing pit stop: try Brew (p54) or Baldry's Tea Room.

(a kind of sophisticated cheese on toast, generously drizzled with a secret ingredient tasting suspiciously like beer), salads and corned beef sandwiches for lunch too.

Crêpes, both savoury and sweet, are the mainstay at **Emma's Dell** (☎015394-35234; www.millerhowecafe.co.uk; Red Lion Sq; mains £4.75-10.50; ⏰8.30am-5.30pm) in the middle of Grasmere. Go classic with melted Nutella, or fill yourself up with cheese and ham.

Husband-and-wife team Andy and Crissy Hill have turned village bistro **Jumble Room** (☎015394-35188; www.thejumbleroom.co.uk; Langdale Rd; dinner mains £14.50-23; ⏰5.30-9.30pm Wed-Mon) into a much-loved dining landmark. It's a really fun and friendly place to eat. Spotty crockery, cow murals and primary colours set the boho tone, matched by a magpie menu that borrows flavours and ingredients from a global cookbook – Malaysian seafood curry one week, Persian lamb the next.

A reliable village bistro, **Lewis's** (☎015394-35266; Broadgate; mains £14.95-24.95; ⏰6-9pm Tue-Sat) turns out hearty, classic British bistro dishes – steak, roast lamb, belly pork, sea bass and the like. It's solid rather than sensational, but a good bet for dinner all the same.

Cheery village cafe **Brew** (☎015394-35248; www.heidisgrasmerelodge.co.uk; Red Lion Sq; mains £4-8; ⏰9am-5.30pm) is the place for a quick lunch of homemade soup and a thick-cut sandwich. The house-special flapjacks and savoury cheese smokeys are sinfully good.

Pleasant **Grasmere Tea Gardens** (☎015394-35590; Stock Lane; ⏰9.30am-5pm) has views of the river

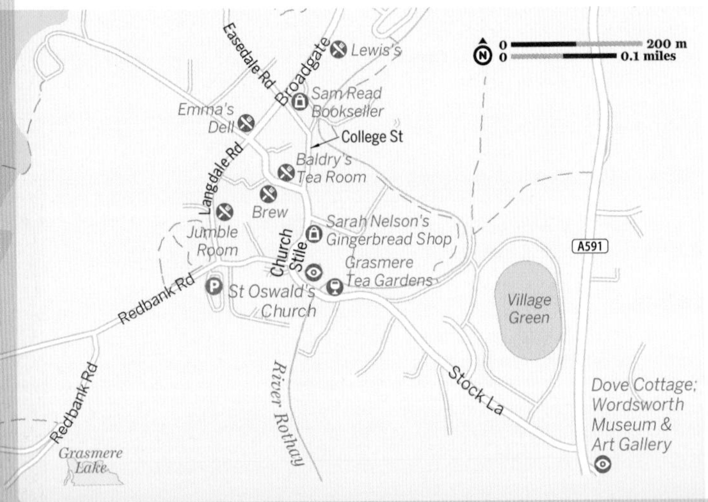

Grasmere Sports Day

Grasmere is fiercely proud of its annual sports day, when local lads and lasses get the chance to test their mettle at a selection of traditional sports on the village green. The event usually takes place on the Sunday of the August Bank Holiday, and has been held practically every year since 1852. In its heyday over 50,000 spectators flocked to the village to enjoy the show; these days audience figures are a more modest 10,000, but the event remains one of the highlights of the Grasmere calendar.

and church – perfect for tea and scones or a slice of posthike cake.

With its sputtering fires and inglenook bar, 16th-century coaching inn **Traveller's Rest** (☎015394-35604; www.lakedistrictinns.co.uk/travellers-rest; A591; ⊙10am-11pm) on the A591 makes a fine place for a pint and a simple pie supper.

Souvenirs

In business since 1854, the famous **Sarah Nelson's Gingerbread Shop** (☎015394-35428; www.grasmeregingerbread.co.uk; Church Cottage; ⊙9.15am-5.30pm Mon-Sat, 12.30-5pm Sun) next to the village church makes Grasmere's essential souvenir: traditional gingerbread with a half-biscuity, half-cakey texture (six/12 pieces for £3.50/6.70), cooked using the original top-secret recipe. Friendly service is provided by ladies dressed in frilly pinafores and starched bonnets.

A bookworm's delight, with a super selection of Lakeland-themed books, **Sam Read Bookseller** (☎015394-35374; http://samreadbooks.moonfruit.com; Broadgate House) also has scores of fiction and nonfiction titles.

Walking Tour

Langdale Pikes

This strenuous walk is the most popular hike in Langdale and crosses over a series of lofty summits, with stirring views over the Langdale and Mickleden Valleys.

Walk Facts

Start New Dungeon Ghyll Hotel; 516 (six daily)

End Old Dungeon Ghyll Hotel; 516

Length 7 miles; six to seven hours

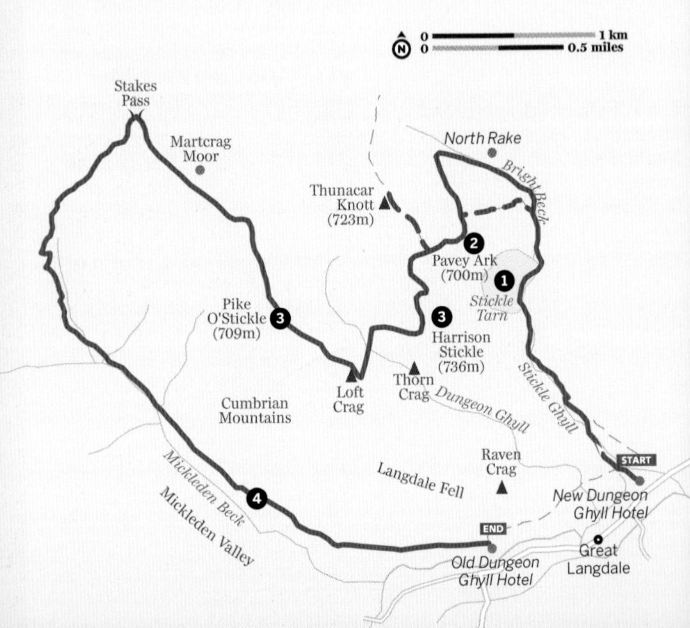

❶ Stickle Tarn

The trail starts behind the **New Dungeon Ghyll Hotel**, leading steeply up past the impressive 40ft tumble of **Dungeon Ghyll Force**, then detouring back up **Stickle Ghyll**. The easiest path starts on the beck's left bank, then crosses over stepping stones halfway up, eventually climbing to **Stickle Tarn**.

❷ Pavey Ark

Take a breather at the tarn and admire the craggy views of your next target, **Pavey Ark**. There are several routes to the summit, including the treacherous scramble up the face of Pavey Ark known as 'Jack's Rake'. A marginally easier scramble leads up Easy Gully, but the most achievable ascent is the route dubbed by Alfred Wainwright as **North Rake**. The trail leads up Bright Beck, and climbs a steep scree gully on its way to the summit; the views are some of the loftiest in Langdale, but take care near the edge.

Pavey Ark is actually an outlying peak of **Thunacar Knott**, so peak-bagging purists will want to head northwest for 500m to the summit. There's no path; just head across the grass for the highest point.

❸ Harrison Stickle & Pike O'Stickle

From here, pick up the well-worn trail along the cliff from Pavey Ark, and follow it to the top of **Harrison Stickle**, at 736m the highest of the Langdale Pikes. From here, the path drops down the fell's west side, climbs over the rubbly ridge of **Loft Crag**, and leads northwest to the distinctive hump of **Pike O' Stickle**. There's a bit of scrambling involved in getting to the top – the drops are daunting but the views are worth it, so take your time and be sure of your footholds.

❹ Mickleden Valley

Once you've conquered the Pikes, follow the faint path across the grassy slopes of **Martcrag Moor** to the junction at **Stakes Pass**. Turn south and follow the zigzagging trail for around 3 miles into the **Mickleden Valley**, ending with a well-deserved posthike pint at the **Old Dungeon Ghyll** (p62), a long-standing hikers' haunt.

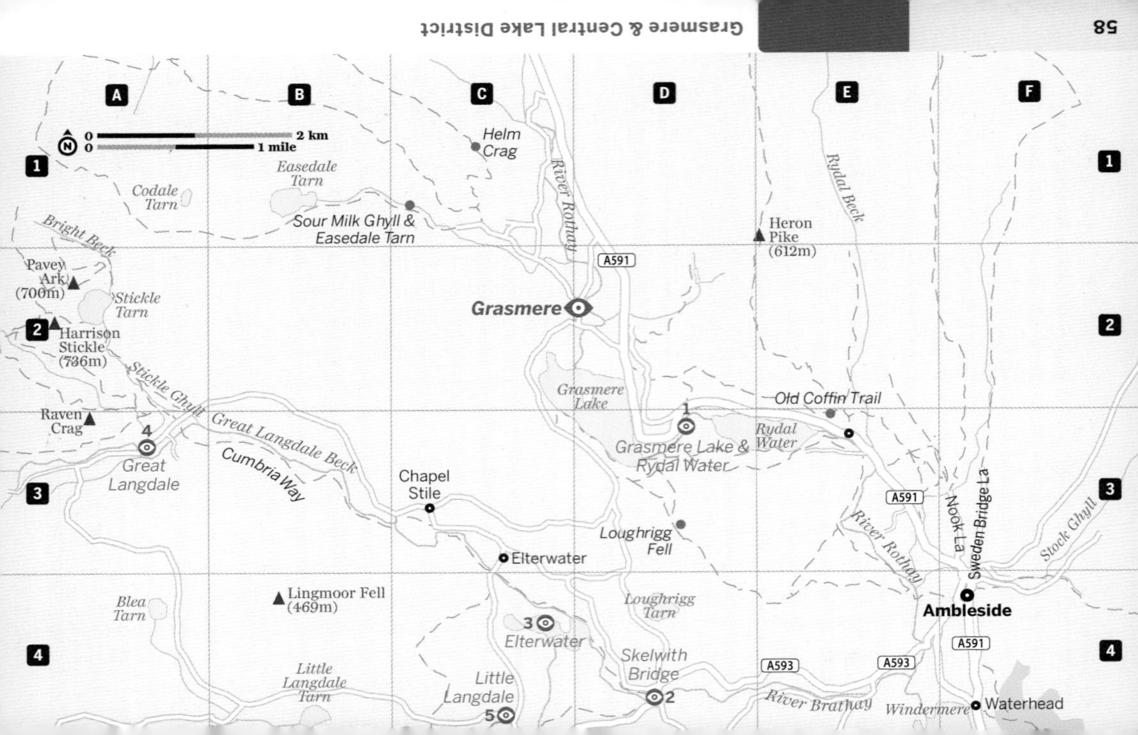
A
B
C
D
E
F
1
2
3
4
0 2 km
0 1 mile
Helm Crag
Easedale Tarn
Codale Tarn
Sour Milk Ghyll & Easedale Tarn
Bright Beck
River Rothay
Rydal Beck
Heron Pike (612m)
A591
Pavey Ark (700m)
Stickle Tarn
Grasmere
Harrison Stickle (736m)
Stickle Ghyll
Grasmere Lake
Old Coffin Trail
Raven Crag
4
Great Langdale Beck
1
Rydal Water
Grasmere Lake & Rydal Water
Great Langdale
Cumbria Way
Chapel Stile
Nook La
Sweden Bridge La
Stock Ghyll
River Rothay
Loughrigg Fell
Elterwater
Ambleside
Lingmoor Fell (469m)
Blea Tarn
Loughrigg Tarn
3
Elterwater
Skelwith Bridge
A593
Little Langdale Tarn
Little Langdale
5
2
River Brathay
Windermere
Waterhead

Grasmere Lake & Rydal Water

1 MAP P58, D3

The poet William Wordsworth's most famous residence in the Lake District is undoubtedly Dove Cottage (p53), but he actually spent a great deal more time at **Rydal Mount** (015394-33002; www.rydalmount.co.uk; adult/child £7.50/4, grounds only £5; 9.30am-5pm Mar-Oct, 11am-4pm Nov, Dec & Feb), 1.5 miles northwest of Ambleside, off the A591. This was the Wordsworth family's home from 1813 until the poet's death in 1850 and the house contains a treasure trove of Wordsworth memorabilia. Bus 555 (and bus 599 from April to October) stops at the end of the drive.

Quiet paths lead along the shores of Grasmere's sparkling twinset of lakes. Rowing boats can be hired at the northern end of Grasmere Lake from the Grasmere Tea Gardens (p54), which is a five-minute walk from the village centre.

For hundreds of years, deceased parishioners from areas around Grasmere were borne to their burials at St Oswald's Church along 'coffin trails' or 'corpse roads'. You can still follow one of them, known as the **Old Coffin Trail**, from just behind Dove Cottage, leading across White Moss Common to the grounds of Rydal Mount; look out for the stone slabs where the coffin-bearers rested their burdens without laying them on the ground. It's a walk of just over a mile, or 45 minutes to an hour.

Helm Crag (p60)

Hiking Around Grasmere

There are some fine walks in the Grasmere area. If you only do one fell walk, make it **Helm Crag**, northwest of the village. Sometimes referred to as 'the Lion and the Lamb', after the twin crags atop its summit, it's a rewarding two-hour climb, but it's dauntingly steep in places, with around 335m of elevation gain. The trail starts on Easedale Rd and is fairly well signposted.

You'll find another good walk option halfway along the footpath along the southern side of Grasmere Lake, where a short, steep path leads straight up to the summit of **Loughrigg Fell** (335m). It may be small, but it packs a mighty punch, with wraparound views encompassing Windermere and the Langdale Pikes. It's a round trip of around two hours from Grasmere.

If you don't feel like a full-on fell walk, the easy path to the clattering waterfall of **Sour Milk Ghyll** and the scenic **Easdale Tarn** is a great option. The path starts at the end of Easedale Rd and leads for about 1.5 miles along Easedale Beck; the first part is paved and wheelchair accessible, but it gets rougher the closer you get to the falls.

Skelwith Bridge

2 MAP P58, D4

Three miles south of Grasmere, Skelwith Bridge is little more than a knot of cottages along the banks of the River Brathay. Since the 19th century it's been a hub for slate quarrying, but these days most people come to walk to **Skelwith Force**, a 15ft tumble of water about 10 minutes' walk from the village. You can extend the walk to nearby **Colwith Force**, which plunges down a series of 46ft-high rock steps about a mile west of the village.

Beside a rattling brook at Skelwith Bridge, halfway between Ambleside and Elterwater, **Chesters by the River** (015394-32553; www.chestersbytheriver.co.uk; lunch mains £8-15; 9am-5pm) is a smart cafe that's definitely more gourmet than greasy spoon: delicious salads, specials and cakes make it well worth a stop. There's a chic gift shop too – items include slate souvenirs from the workshop around the corner.

Elterwater

3 MAP P58, C3

Named by Norse settlers after the colonies of whooper swans that still swoop across its surface every winter, **Elterwater** (literally 'Swan Lake') presents the picture-postcard image of a traditional Lakeland village, with its tree-fringed lake and clump of slate-roofed cottages gathered around a maple-shaded village green. Somewhat bizarrely for such a peaceful spot, Elterwater originally grew up around the industries of slate quarrying, farming and gunpowder manufacture. Various trails wind out along the lake shore.

Charming **Eltermere Inn** (015394-37207; www.eltermere.co.uk; r £149-295; P) is one of Lakeland's loveliest backwater boltholes. The food is excellent, served in the inn's snug bar; afternoon tea is served on the lawn on sunny days. If you want to stay the night, rooms are simple and classic, tastefully decorated in fawns and taupes with quirky features such as window seats and free-standing baths.

On Elterwater's village green, the classic whitewashed **Britannia Inn** (015394-37210; www.thebritanniainn.com; 11am-11pm) has been serving ale for five centuries: the current line-up includes brews from Coniston Brewery and the nearby Langdale Brewing Company (our pick is the superbly named Neddy Boggle Bitter). There are nooks and crannies aplenty to hunker down in, and tables on the grassy lawn out front for sunny days.

Great Langdale

4 MAP P58, A3

The wild, empty landscape of Great Langdale is one of Lakeland's

Slater's Bridge (p63)

iconic hiking valleys (see p56). Luckily, there are some good spots to restore your energy after your exertions.

Now run by the National Trust and housed in a converted barn, **Sticklebarn** (015394-37356; mains lunch £5-8, dinner £11-13.50; 11am-9pm) is a walkers' favourite: it's packed with people nursing pints and aching fell-sore legs at the end of the day. Food is wholesome and hearty: Herdwick lamb and ale stew, venison *ragu* and *ropa vieja* chilli, washed down with a good ale selection.

Affectionately known as the ODG, **Old Dungeon Ghyll** (015394-37272; www.odg.co.uk; s £58, d £116-132; P) is awash with Lakeland heritage: many famous walkers have stayed at this inn, including Prince Charles and mountaineer Chris Bonington. It's endearingly olde worlde (well-worn furniture, four-poster beds) and even if you're not staying, the slate-floored, fire-warmed Hiker's Bar is a must for a posthike pint – it's been the hub of Langdale's social life for decades.

Little Langdale

5 MAP P58, C4

Separated from Great Langdale by the hefty bulk of Lingmoor Fell (469m/1540ft), the valley of **Little Langdale** traditionally marks the juncture between the old counties of Cumberland, Westmorland and Lancashire – a point officially marked by the **Three Shire Stone**, positioned near the steep summit of Wrynose Pass. The stone was broken into bits when it was hit by a wayward motorist in 1997; it was restored the following year by a local stonemason thanks to the

Parking in Langdale

Hiking is very much the main attraction in Great Langdale, but it's a notoriously popular spot – during the summer you might well find that all the parking spaces at the official car parks are gone by 10am. There are National Trust car parks at Stickle Ghyll and the Old Dungeon Ghyll Hotel (free for NT members), plus one run by the National Park Authority (NPA) opposite the New Dungeon Ghyll.

Roadside parking isn't allowed in the valley, so to cope with demand, there are a couple of unofficial car parks in privately owned fields that open in summer.

Many people find it easier to follow in fell-walker and author Alfred Wainwright's footsteps and clamber aboard the Langdale Rambler bus instead, which trundles up and down the valley six times a day during the high season.

The Langdale Axe Factory

High up on the scree slopes beneath Pike O' Stickle and Harrison Stickle in Great Langdale is one of the largest neolithic **axe factories** in Britain. The area has rich deposits of a form of greenstone, a hard form of volcanic stone that can be worked to a fine, sharp edge. Early craftsmen selected their stones carefully, shaped them roughly on the fellside, then spent many hours honing and polishing them: hundreds of 'reject' heads still litter the quarry site. Around 27% of all the neolithic axes discovered in Britain are thought to have originated from Langdale, with examples found as far afield as Ireland and Cornwall.

generous donations of Langdale residents and the National Trust.

The valley is a popular hiking base, with several possible destinations including Blea Tarn, Little Langdale Tarn and Lingmoor Fell. For a shorter stroll, it's well worth taking the short path from the Three Shires Inn to **Slater's Bridge**, a pretty little 17th-century humpback bridge once used by workers carrying slate from the nearby slate quarry of Cathedral Cavern.

Beyond the pub, the road crawls up to the high passes of **Wrynose** and **Hardknott** before dropping down into Eskdale en route to the Cumbrian Coast. See p124 for our Wrynose and Hardknott driving tour.

Hill Top, Coniston & Hawkshead

Windermere is bigger, Wastwater is wilder, but Coniston Water maintains an air of serenity even on the busiest days. It's one of the prettiest corners of the Lakes – a postcard patchwork of woodlands, valleys, villages and cottages, including Beatrix Potter's world-famous home at Hill Top, in the village of Near Sawrey.

Kick off with a morning cruise on the stately Steam Yacht Gondola (p72) to John Ruskin's fascinating former home at Brantwood (p75). Have lunch at the house's own cafe, or catch the boat back for tea and cake at Herdwicks (p71). Spend the afternoon walking the trails around Tarn Hows (p77) or Grizedale Forest (p77) before making a late visit to Hill Top (p66), ideally when the crowds have left for home. Have an early evening pint at the Black Bull (p71), followed by dinner in Coniston at Steam Bistro (p71) or the superb Drunken Duck (p76) on nearby Hawkshead Hill.

Getting There & Around

Bus 505 runs from Windermere via Hawkshead and Ambleside.

Two ferries run across Coniston Water: the Coniston Launch (p72) and the Steam Yacht Gondola (p72). The Coniston Bus-and-Boat ticket (p71) includes Brantwood.

The B5285 runs west from Hawkshead to Coniston, south to Grizedale Forest, and southeast to Near Sawrey and Ferry House, the western dock for the Windermere Ferry.

Hill Top, Coniston & Hawkshead Map on p70

Brantwood (p75)

Top Sights

Hill Top

Two miles south of Hawkshead, in the tiny village of Near Sawrey, this idyllic farmhouse was purchased in 1905 by Beatrix Potter and served as a model for many of her tales. It's one of the most popular sights in the Lakes, so expect crowds.

MAP P70, E4

015394-36269

www.nationaltrust.org.uk/hill-top

adult/child £10.90/5.45

10am-5.30pm Jun-Aug, to 4.30pm Sat-Thu Apr, May, Sep & Oct, weekends only Nov-Mar

The History of Hill Top

Clad in climbing ivy and stocked with memorabilia, Hill Top looks, appropriately enough, like something out of a story book. Many visitors assume Beatrix lived her entire life here, but although it was her first permanent Lake District home, she was already nearly 40 by the time she bought it, and only lived here full-time following her marriage to the local solicitor William Heelis. In 1913 the couple moved to a larger farm at nearby Castle Cottage, where the author wrote many more tales until her death in 1943, although she kept Hill Top for the rest of her life.

After her death in 1943, she bequeathed the house (along with Castle Cottage and more than 1600 hectares of land) to the National Trust, with the proviso that the house should be left with her belongings and decor in situ.

The House

Beatrix was an inveterate collector, and the house is crammed with a huge collection of antiques, curios and objets d'art collected during her lifetime. Among the collection you'll see antique fans, doll's houses, painted chinaware and butterfly collections, as well as Beatrix' own paint tin, the handkerchief that supposedly inspired the one worn by Benjamin Bunny, and of course lots of original illustrations. But it's the house itself that's most fascinating – scholarly Potterites will be able to spot decorative details from practically every tale in the canon.

The Garden

The garden at Hill Top was planned (and largely planted) under Beatrix's close supervision, and served regularly as a backdrop for her tales – most notably in *Peter Rabbit* and *Tom Kitten*. It's beautifully planted, and, of course, there's a well-stocked allotment that Mr McGregor himself would be proud of.

★ Top Tips

- Hill Top is incredibly popular – it's one of the must-see places for nearly every visitor to the Lakes.
- All visits are conducted within specific time slots – but you can't prebook, and tickets often sell out.
- Try visiting in the late afternoon or on weekdays to avoid the worst crowds.

Take a Break

Practically next door to Hill Top, the **Tower Bank Arms** (☎ 015394-36334; www.towerbankarms.co.uk; Near Sawrey; mains £8-14) famously featured in *The Tale of Jemima Puddle-Duck*. Covered in climbing roses and with a neat little clock above the porch, it makes a fine spot for lunch. There's a sweet little beer garden out back.

Walking Tour

Old Man of Coniston

Hunkering above Coniston like a benevolent giant, the Old Man (803m) presents an irresistible challenge. The most popular route up the Old Man is straight up from Coniston, tackling the east side up through the Coppermines Valley. But it's a leg-sappingly steep slog – this route circles behind the Old Man via the ridge between Brown Pike and Dow Crag.

Walk Facts

Start Coniston; 505

End Coniston

Length 7½ miles; four to five hours

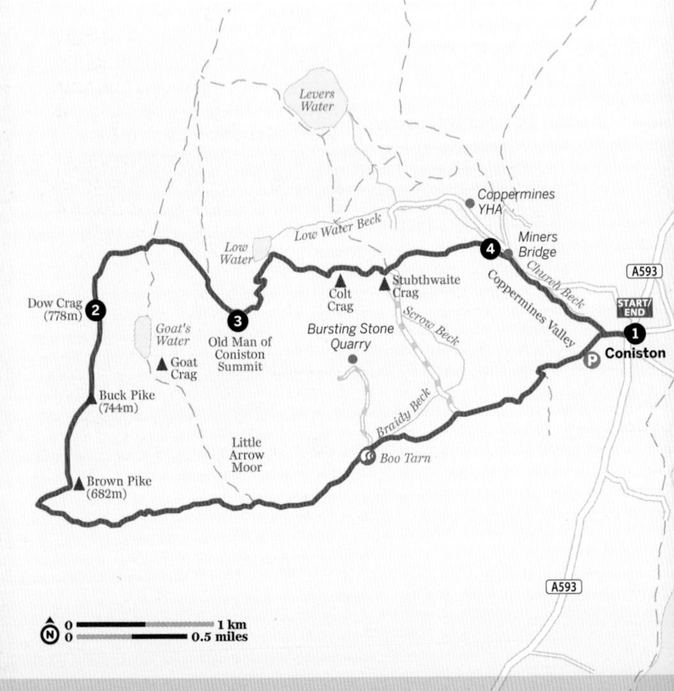

❶ Coniston to Walna Scar Road

Start in **Coniston** and follow the road past the **Sun Hotel** (p71) for half a mile to the start of **Walna Scar Rd** (you can park here if you've got a car). Go through the gate and head west along the track, admiring the view across the barren expanse of **Torver High Common**.

❷ Dow Crag

The path leads west, passing the tiny pond of **Boo Tarn** after about a mile. Ignore the side-trail north towards Goat's Water and continue west, following the trail up as it climbs the south flank of **Brown Pike** (682m) and traces the ridgeline across **Buck Pike** (744m) and **Dow Crag** (778m). The views east across Goat's Water to the Old Man are superb, but the drop is severe; take care near the edge, especially when it's windy.

❸ Old Man of Coniston Summit

From Dow Crag, the trail circles round the northern side of **Goat's Water**, dropping into the saddle of **Goat's Hause** before following a leg-sapping incline up the west side of the Old Man. At the **summit** you'll be rewarded with a glorious 360-degree panorama, east over Coniston Water, north towards Wetherlam and west towards the trio of fells you've just climbed. On a clear day, you'll see south all the way to Morecambe Bay.

❹ Coppermines Valley

From the cairn at the top, a zigzag trail tracks sharply down the mountain's northern side. Follow the slippery path down to **Low Water**, and then east through the abandoned slate quarries beneath Colt Crag; a stone staircase has been cut out at points, but it's still very steep. The path winds down the valley along the southern back of Levers Beck, passing the **Coppermines YHA** (☎0845-371 9630; www.yha.org.uk; dm from £16; ⏰reception 7-11am & 5-10pm Easter-Oct) en route back to the village.

✕ Take a Break

Once back in Coniston, you've earned a hearty lunch at Herdwicks (p71), or a restorative pint at the Black Bull (p71).

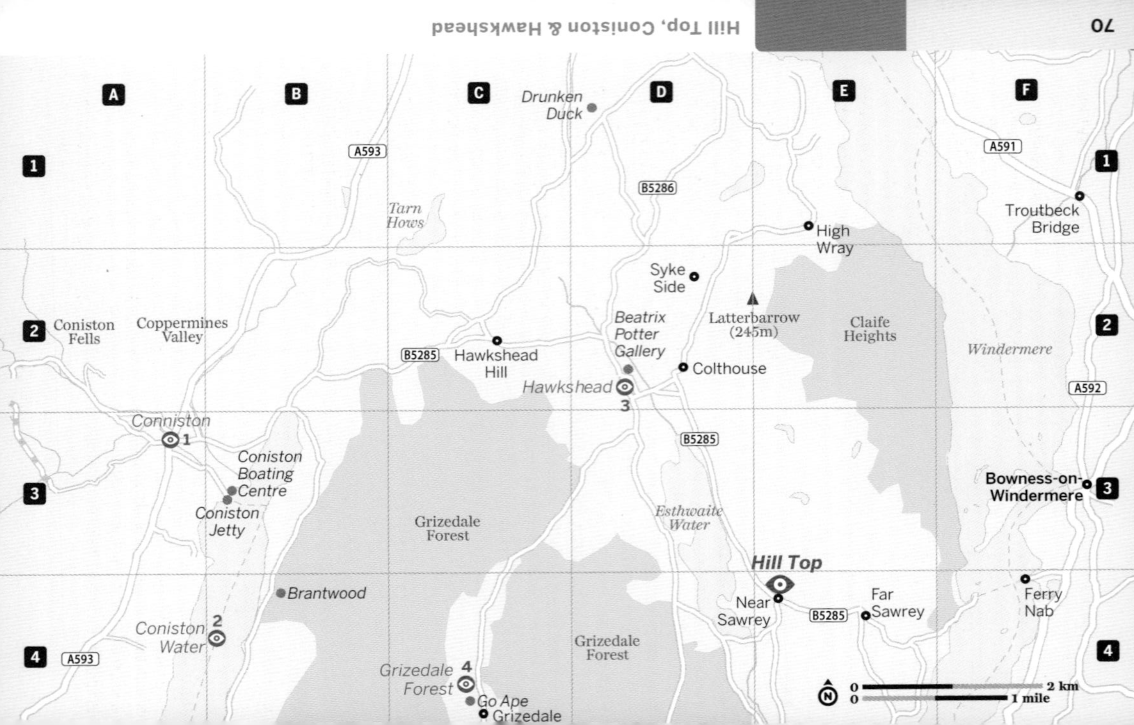
A
B
C
D
E
F
1
2
3
4
Drunken Duck
A593
B5286
A591
Tarn Hows
High Wray
Troutbeck Bridge
Syke Side
Coniston Fells
Coppermines Valley
Beatrix Potter Gallery
Latterbarrow (245m)
Claife Heights
Windermere
B5285
Hawkshead Hill
Colthouse
Hawkshead
A592
Conniston
Coniston Boating Centre
Coniston Jetty
Grizedale Forest
Esthwaite Water
Bowness-on-Windermere
Hill Top
Brantwood
Near Sawrey
Far Sawrey
Ferry Nab
Coniston Water
Grizedale Forest
Go Ape
Grizedale
0
2 km
1 mile

Coniston Village

1 MAP 70, A3

The lakeside village of Coniston was originally established to support the local mining industry, and the surrounding hilltops are littered with the remains of old copper workings. Recover here after conquering the Old Man of Coniston (p68), or explore on your way to Coniston Water (p72).

The little **Ruskin Museum** (015394-41164; www.ruskinmuseum.com; adult/child £6/3; 10am-4.30pm mid-Mar–mid-Nov) explores the village's history, touching on copper mining, Arthur Ransome and the Campbell story (p74). There's also a section on John Ruskin, who lived at nearby Brantwood (p75), with displays of his writings, watercolours and sketchbooks. It's also closely connected to the decade-long project to rebuild Donald Campbell's *Bluebird K7*, with various pieces of the remodelled boat on display; find out more about the project at www.bluebirdproject.com.

Coniston offers some good eating and drinking options.

Run by a local family, the bright and cheery cafe **Herdwicks** (015394-41141; Yewdale Rd; mains £4-10; 10am-4pm) makes the perfect stop for lunch – whether you're in the mood for homemade soup, a big chunky sandwich, or a slice of sinful cake. Everything is locally sourced where possible, and the light-filled, large-windowed space is inviting.

The swish new **Steam Bistro** (015394-41928; www.steambistro.co.uk; Tilberthwaite Ave; 2-/3-course menu £22.95/26.95; 6-11pm Wed-Sun) has become the go-to address for Coniston dining. Its magpie menu borrows lots of global flavours – you'll find everything from Japanese dumplings to Cajun pulled pork and Greek-style *kleftiko* (slow-cooked lamb) on the specials board. Even better, everything is *prix fixe* (fixed price).

Famously used as a headquarters by Donald Campbell during his fateful campaign, the trad boozer **Sun Hotel** (015394-41248; www.thesunconiston.com; 10am-11pm) is a good place for a pint, with a fell-view beer garden and cosy crannies to hunker down in – look out for Campbell memorabilia. Food (mains £12 to £21) is hit-and-miss at busy times. It's up a small hill beside the bridge over Church Beck.

Coniston's main meeting spot, the old **Black Bull** (015394-41335; www.conistonbrewery.com/black-bull-coniston.htm; Yewdale Rd; 10am-11pm) offers a warren of

Coniston Bus-&-Boat Ticket

The Coniston Bus-and-Boat ticket (adult/child £19/8.30) includes return bus travel on the 505, plus a trip on the launch and entry to Brantwood.

rooms and a popular outside terrace. The pub grub's good (mains £8 to £18), but it's mainly known for its home-brewed ales: Bluebird Bitter and Old Man Ale are always on tap and there are seasonal ones too.

Coniston Water

2 MAP 70, B4

The gleaming 5-mile-long lake of Coniston Water – the third largest in the Lake District after Windermere and Ullswater – is a half-mile walk from the village of Coniston along Lake Rd.

The best way to explore the lake itself is on one of the two cruise services. Built in 1859 and restored in the 1980s by the National Trust, the wonderful **Steam Yacht Gondola** (NT; ☎015394-63850; www.nationaltrust.org.uk/steam-yacht-gondola; Coniston Jetty; half lake adult/child/family £11/6/25, full lake adult/child/family £21/10/48) looks like a cross between a Venetian *vaporetto* and an English houseboat, complete with cushioned saloons and polished wood seats. It's a stately way to see the lake, especially if you're visiting Brantwood, and it's ecofriendly – since 2008 it's been powered by waste wood.

Coniston Launch (☎015394-36216; www.conistonlaunch.co.uk; Coniston Jetty; adult/child return Red Route £11.50/5.75, Yellow Route £12.75/6.40, Green Route £17.25/8.65) operates two modern launches, which have been solar-powered since 2005. The regular 45-minute **Northern Service (Red Route)**

Coniston Water

The Tale of Beatrix Potter

Of all the Lake District's literary figures, none commands a more fanatical following than Helen Beatrix Potter (1866–1943). More than a century after the publication of her first book, *The Tale of Peter Rabbit*, her anthropomorphic children's fables continue to sell by the bucketload, and her former house at Hill Top (p66) remains one of the most visited tourist attractions in northern England, receiving in excess of 65,000 visitors every year.

Born to a privileged family in South Kensington in 1866, Beatrix Potter's connections with the Lake District date back to a family holiday in 1882. A shy, lonely child, the young Beatrix became fascinated by animals, botany and nature, whiling away hours sketching flowers, trees and fungi, not to mention a menagerie of pets: frogs, newts, toads and ferrets, as well as a pair of bunny rabbits named Peter and Benjamin Bouncer (who she liked to parade around on a lead).

Beatrix was encouraged to pursue her artistic ambitions by the local vicar and family friend Canon Hardwicke Rawnsley. Her first book, *The Tale of Peter Rabbit, was* initially rejected by several publishers, but eventually published by the small firm Frederick Warne & Co in 1901. It was a smash hit, selling in excess of 25,000 copies in its first year. Its financial success enabled Potter to buy Hill Top – the first of many property purchases in the Lakes – and spawned 22 more books over the next 20 years, culminating with *The Tale of Little Pig Robinson* in 1930.

Her first engagement to her publisher, Norman Warne, ended tragically in 1905 when he died of anaemia. She later married the local solicitor William Heelis in 1913. After her marriage, Beatrix became increasingly interested in hill-farming and animal husbandry. During the 1920s and '30s, she established her own prize-winning flock of Herdwick sheep, became president of the Herdwick Sheep Breeders' Association, and worked tirelessly to protect the Lakeland landscape she so adored.

She died in 1943 at the age of 77, bequeathing her 1600-hectare estate to the National Trust. Some of her early work is displayed at the Armitt Museum (p46) in Ambleside and the Beatrix Potter Gallery (p76) in Hawkshead.

Speed: The Campbell Story

Between the 1930s and the 1960s, Coniston Water was the unlikely setting for a series of audacious attempts to break the world water-speed record by Sir Malcolm Campbell and his son, Donald.

Coniston's speed connections stretch back to the late 1930s, when Malcolm (already a national motorcycle champion, Grand Prix racer and holder of nine land-speed records) chose the lake for an attempt on the water-speed record, which he had already broken three times (on Lake Geneva, Lake Maggiore in Italy and Lake Halwell in Switzerland). On 19 August 1939, piloting the jet-fuelled powerboat *Bluebird K4*, Campbell reached 141.74mph – a record that was intact a decade later when he died at home in Surrey in 1948.

In June 1950 Malcolm's record was finally broken by the American pilot Stan Sayers, who achieved a new speed of 160.32mph in his boat *Slo-mo-shun IV*. Malcolm's son, ex-RAF pilot Donald Campbell, subsequently regained his father's record in 1955 in *Bluebird K7* – reaching 202.32mph on Ullswater, followed the same year by 216.1mph at Lake Mead in the USA. Donald smashed the water-speed record several more times over the next decade, culminating in 1964 at Lake Dumbleyung in Western Australia, where he reached 276.3mph, having already achieved the land-speed record (403.1mph) a year before.

Tragically, the Campbell story ended in disaster on Coniston Water on 4 January 1967. Having already clocked 297mph, Donald made another attempt without allowing time for the wake from his previous run to subside. Near the end of his return run, at an estimated 328mph, the *Bluebird's* bow rose out of the water, flipped and struck the lake nose-first, killing Donald instantly. Thirty seconds later the boat had sunk without trace.

After resting on the lake-bed for more than three decades, the remains of the boat and its pilot were recovered in March 2001. Donald was buried in the village churchyard of St Andrews, and the boat itself is currently being restored (hopefully to full working order) by the local engineer and wreck diver, Bill Smith, with the blessing of Campbell's daughter Gina. Find out the latest news on the restoration at www.bluebirdproject.com.

calls at the Waterhead Hotel, Torver and Brantwood. The 60-minute **Wild Cat Island Cruise (Yellow Route)** tours the lake's islands. The 105-minute **Southern Service (Green Route)** is themed: it's Swallows and Amazons on Monday and Wednesday, and the Campbell story on Tuesday and Thursday.

Better still, paddle the lake yourself. Dinghies, rowing boats, canoes, kayaks and motor boats can be hired from **Coniston Boating Centre** (Map p70; ☎015394-41366; www.conistonboatingcentre.co.uk; Coniston Jetty). Try out rowing boats (£15 per hour), kayaks and stand-up paddleboards (£20 for two hours), Canadian canoes (£25 for two hours) and motor boats (£30 per hour). It also rents out bikes (adult/child £15/5 for two hours).

To refuel lakeside, the **Bluebird Cafe** (☎015394-41649; Lake Rd; mains £4-8; ⏰9.30am-5.30pm) does a brisk trade from people waiting for the Coniston launches. The usual salads, jacket spuds and sandwiches are on offer and there are lots of tables outside where you can look out on the lake.

On the eastern side of the lake is John Ruskin's home, **Brantwood** (Map p70; ☎015394-41396; www.brantwood.org.uk; adult/child £7.70/free, gardens only £5.35/free; ⏰10.30am-5pm mid-Mar–mid-Nov, to 4pm Wed-Sun mid-Nov–mid-Mar). John Ruskin (1819–1900) was one of the great thinkers of 19th-century society. A polymath, philosopher, painter and critic, he expounded views on everything from Venetian architecture to lacemaking. In 1871

Hawkshead Grammar School (p76)

Ruskin purchased this lakeside house and spent the next 20 years modifying it, championing handmade crafts (he even designed the wallpaper). Look out for his vast shell collection. Boats run regularly to Brantwood from Coniston. Alternatively, look out for signs on the B5285.

Hawkshead

3 MAP 70, D2

Pint-sized Hawkshead is a jumble of whitewashed cottages, cobbled lanes and old pubs lost among bottle-green countryside between Ambleside and Coniston. It has plenty of literary cachet too.

Start with a visit to the **Beatrix Potter Gallery** (Map p70; NT; www.nationaltrust.org.uk/beatrix-potter-gallery; Red Lion Sq; adult/child £6.50/3.25; 10.30am-5pm Sat-Thu mid-Mar–Oct). As well as being a children's author, Beatrix Potter was also a talented botanical painter and amateur naturalist. This small gallery, housed in what were once the offices of Potter's husband, solicitor William Heelis, contains a collection of her watercolours depicting local flora and fauna. She was particularly fascinated by mushrooms.

Continue the literary connections at **Hawkshead Grammar School** (www.hawksheadgrammar.org.uk; £2.50; 10.30am-1pm & 1.30-5pm Mon-Sat Apr-Oct). In centuries past, promising young gentlemen were sent to Hawkshead's village school for their educational foundation. Among the former pupils was a certain William Wordsworth, who attended the school from 1779 to 1787 – you can still see a desk where the naughty young poet carved his name. The curriculum was punishing: 10 hours' study a day, covering weighty subjects such as Latin, Greek, geometry, science and rhetoric. Upstairs is a small exhibition exploring the history of the school.

The best choice of several pubs in Hawkshead is **Queen's Head** (015394-36271; www.queensheadhawkshead.co.uk; Main St; mains £12-15; noon-3pm & 6-10pm), with

Deluxe Dining: Drunken Duck

Long one of the Lakes' premier dining destinations, the **Drunken Duck** (Map p70; 015394-36347; www.drunkenduckinn.co.uk; Barngates; lunch/dinner mains £10/22; noon-2pm & 6-10pm; P) blends historic pub and fine-dining restaurant. On a wooded crossroads on the top of Hawkshead Hill, it's renowned for its luxurious food and home-brewed ales, and the flagstones and sporting prints conjure a convincing country atmosphere. Book well ahead for dinner or take your chances at lunchtime.

Beauty Spot: Tarn Hows

Two miles off the B5285 from Hawkshead, a winding country lane leads to **Tarn Hows** (Map p70; NT; www.nationaltrust.org.uk/coniston-and-tarn-hows), a famously photogenic artificial lake, now owned by the National Trust. Trails wind their way around the lakeshore and surrounding woodland – keep your eyes peeled for red squirrels in the treetops.

the requisite head-knockingly low ceilings and oak-panelled walls. Decent food plus pleasant four-poster rooms (£100 to £170) above, with more in a modern annexe.

For a tasty addition to a picnic, visit the **Hawkshead Relish Company** (☎015394-36614; www.hawksheadrelish.com; The Square; ⌚9.30am-5pm winter, 9am-5.30pm summer), which sells an enormous choice of relishes and jams.

Grizedale Forest

4 MAP 70, C4

Stretching for 2428 hectares across the hilltops between Coniston Water and Esthwaite Water is Grizedale Forest (www.forestry.gov.uk/grizedale), a dense conifer forest whose name derives from the Old Norse 'griss-dale', meaning 'valley of the pigs'.

The forest has nine walking trails and seven cycling trails to explore – some are easy and designed for families, while others are geared towards hard-core hikers and cyclists. Along the way you'll spot more than 40 outdoor sculptures hidden in the undergrowth, created by artists since 1977 (there's a useful online guide at www.grizedalesculpture.org).

Trail maps are sold at the visitors centre, while bikes can be hired from **Grizedale Mountain Bikes** (☎01229-860335; www.grizedalemountainbikes.co.uk; adult/child per half-day from £25/15; ⌚9am-5pm).

For some adventure in the forest, **Go Ape** (Map p70; www.goape.co.uk/days-out/grizedale; adult/child £33/25; ⌚9am-5pm daily Mar-Oct, Sat & Sun Nov-Feb; 👪) is part of a national chain of woodland assault courses. There are several ways to get your thrills here, from Tarzan swings and rope ladders to a Zip Trekking Adventure involving seven tandem zip wires. It's in the middle of Grizedale Forest and well signposted. There's a minimum age of 10 years for mini-baboons.

Explore

Keswick & Derwentwater

The most northerly of the Lake District's major towns, Keswick has perhaps the most beautiful location of all: encircled by cloud-capped fells and nestled alongside the island-studded lake of Derwentwater. It's also ideal for exploring the nearby valleys of Borrowdale and Buttermere, and a great base for walking – the fells of Skiddaw and Blencathra rise nearby.

After an early breakfast, stroll down to the Derwentwater jetties for the first cruise of the day on the Keswick Launch (p90). Hop off at Hawse End jetty for a hike up Catbells (p91), then catch the boat back to Keswick for lunch at Fellpack (p81). While away the afternoon exploring town, with visits to Keswick Museum (p81) and the Derwent Pencil Museum (p81), and a bit of shopping at the Lake District's oldest (and best) outdoors store, George Fisher (p83). Finish with pizza and drinks at Square Orange (p82) or, for something fancier, Morrels (p83) or the nearby Cottage in the Woods (p92).

Getting There & Around

Bus 555/556 Lakeslink runs hourly to Grasmere, Ambleside, Windermere and Kendal. The 77/77A follows a circular route from Keswick via Borrowdale, Honister Pass, Buttermere and Whinlatter. The hourly 78 just serves Borrowdale.

The busy A66 bypass travels north of Keswick. The B5289 runs south from Keswick into Borrowdale, over Honister Pass, drops into Buttermere, then loops back towards Keswick over the Whinlatter Pass.

Keswick & Derwentwater Map on p88

View of Keswick (p80) from Catbells MATT ROBINSON/500PX ©

Top Sights

Keswick

Nestled at the head of Derwentwater among a group of towering fells, Keswick is one of the handsomest of all the Lake District's market towns. Centred on a lively cobbled marketplace crammed with enough outdoors stores to launch an assault on Everest, the town is the northern Lakes' main commercial centre – so don't be surprised if you encounter some crowds in the summer.

MAP P88, F3

www.keswick.org

Village Sights & Activities

Quirky **Keswick Museum** (pictured; ☎017687-73263; www.keswickmuseum.org.uk; Station Rd; adult/child £4.50/3; ⏰10am-4pm) explores the area's history, from ancient archaeology through to the arrival of industry in the Lakes. It's a diverse collection, taking in everything from neolithic axe heads mined in the Langdale valley to a huge collection of taxidermied butterflies. Its best-known exhibits are a 700-year-old mummified cat and the Musical Stones of Skiddaw, a weird instrument made from hornsfel rock that was once played for Queen Victoria.

Reopened after being badly damaged in the 2015 floods, Keswick's oddest museum, **Derwent Pencil Museum** (☎017687-73626; www.pencilmuseum.co.uk; Southy Works; adult/child £4.95/3.95; ⏰9.30am-5pm) is devoted to the charms of the humble pencil. Exhibits include a pencil made for the Queen's Diamond Jubilee, wartime spy pencils that were hollowed out for secret maps, and the world's largest pencil (a mighty 8m long). It all stems from the discovery of graphite in the Borrowdale valley during the 17th century, after which Keswick became a major pencil manufacturer.

Also in the village, **Keswick Adventure Centre** (☎017687-75687; www.keswickadventurecentre.co.uk; Newlands) organises hikes and has a climbing wall.

Standouts for Food Lovers

There's no shortage of spots for a bite to eat in charming Keswick.

On-trend cafe **Fellpack** (☎017687-71177; www.fellpack.co.uk; 19 Lake Rd; lunches £4-8; ⏰10am-4pm Wed-Mon, 6-9pm Thu-Sat) specialises in 'fell pots' – a Lakeland-style Buddha bowl, incorporating an all-in-one meal such as sweet potato and curry, smoked macaroni and peas, or braised chilli beef, all freshly made and flavour-packed. Flatbreads and baguettes are offered

★ Top Tips

Keswick has one of the busiest calendars in the Lake District. Highlights include the following:

Keswick Mountain Festival (www.keswickmountainfestival.co.uk) Mid-May

Keswick Jazz Festival (www.keswickjazzfestival.co.uk) Mid-May

Keswick Beer Festival (www.keswickbeerfestival.co.uk) June.

for lunch to go. The owners are full of enthusiasm and the food is zingy and imaginative. We like it. It's also open three nights a week for dinner.

Dog fans rejoice: **Jasper's Coffee House** (☎017687-73366; 20 Station St; sandwiches from £4, dishes £6-8; ⏰10am-4pm Mon-Thu, 9am-5pm Fri-Sun; 🐾) is nuts about canines. Dishes here are named after dogs of legend (The Muttley, The Old Yeller, The Huckleberry Hound), there are doggie prints on the walls, and naturally, canine companions are welcome. Foodwise, it's standard brunch-lunch fare: pittas, sausage rolls, wraps and sandwiches, and cooked breakfasts.

On the top floor of George Fisher, **Abrahams' Tea Rooms** (☎017687-72178; www.georgefisher.co.uk/cafe; 2 Borrowdale Rd; mains £6-10; ⏰10am-5pm Mon-Sat, 10.30am-4.30pm Sun) is great for a country lunch: try hot rarebit (toasted cheese on toast), mackerel pâté or a classic baked spud. The space was once occupied by the Abraham brothers, early pioneers of Lakeland photography.

For a sweet treat, try **Bryson's** (42 Main St; cakes £2-5; ⏰8.30am-5.30pm), an old-fashioned and much-loved bakery known for its delicious fruit cakes, Battenbergs and Florentines.

Lively **Square Orange** (☎017687-73888; www.thesquareorange.co.uk; 20 St John's St; ⏰10am-11pm Sun-Thu, to midnight Fri & Sat) seems to have become everyone's favourite hang-out in Keswick – thanks no doubt to its superb thin-based pizzas, excellent wine and craft-beer selection and a regular programme of live gigs. With its big wooden bar and packed-in tables, it feels rather continental –

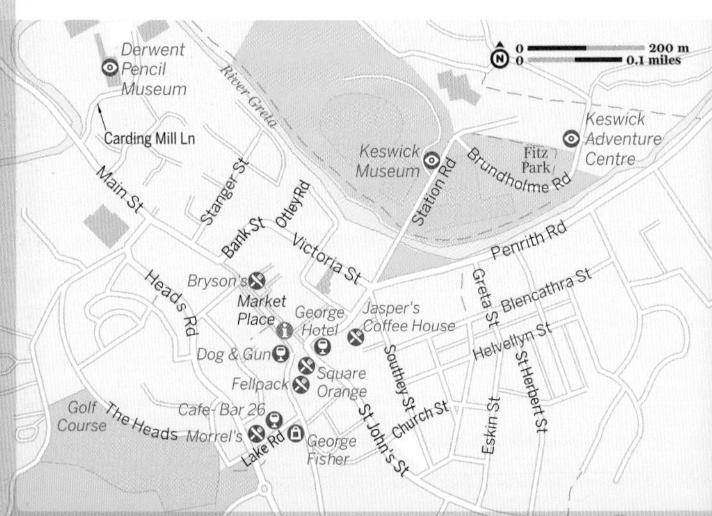

Get into Gear

Quite possibly the most famous outdoors shop in the Lake District, **George Fisher** (017687-72178; www.georgefisher.co.uk; 2 Borrowdale Rd; 9am-5.30pm Mon-Sat, 10am-4pm Sun) was founded in 1967 and still the place where discerning hikers go to buy their gear (even if it is a bit more expensive than the chains). There are three floors of boots, tents and gear, and the boot-fitting service is legendarily thorough.

and the coffee is hands down the best in Keswick.

Probably the best option in Keswick for a sit-down dinner, **Morrel's** (017687-72666; www.morrels.co.uk; Lake Rd; 3-course menu £21.95, mains £12.50-22.50; 5.30-9pm Tue-Sun) is an attractive restaurant majoring in British bistro-style food. Glossy wood, spotlights and glass give it a refined feel.

Whet Your Whistle

Options abound for a pint or two in Keswick.

A spit-and-sawdust pub that claims to be the oldest drinking den in town, **George Hotel** (017687-72076; www.georgehotelkeswick.co.uk; St John's St; 11am-11pm) is owned by Jenning's Brewery. You can sup on a pint of Cumberland or Sneck Lifter while you make pals with the locals.

The old **Dog & Gun** (017687-73463; 2 Lake Rd; 11am-11pm) is the picture of a Lakeland pub with benches, beams, hearths and rugs. Look out for Thirst Rescue ale, which donates part of its proceeds to the Keswick Mountain Rescue Team.

A cosy corner wine bar, **Cafe-Bar 26** (017687-80863; 26 Lake Rd; 9am-11pm Mon-Sat, 10am-10pm Sun) also serves good lunches and evening tapas (£4 to £10).

Top Sights

Borrowdale & Buttermere

With their patchwork of craggy hills, broad fields, tinkling streams and drystone walls, the side-by-side valleys of Borrowdale and Buttermere are many people's idea of the quintessential Lakeland landscape. Once a centre for mineral mining (especially slate, coal and graphite), this is walkers' country these days and, apart from the odd rickety barn or puttering tractor, there's precious little to spoil the view.

MAP P88, F5, D5

017687-72645

www.keswick.org

Moot Hall, Market Pl

9.30am-4.30pm

Borrowdale

Running from the southern edge of Derwentwater to the high point of Honister Pass, the valley of Borrowdale is one of the most beautiful in the Lakes. From Keswick, head along the B5289 into Borrowdale. First stop is Lodore Falls (p92), a pretty cascade at the southern end of Derwentwater. Next, detour to the little hamlet of **Grange-in-Borrowdale** (pictured), where a trail leads up the slate-strewn sides of Castle Crag (p91), a small fell with great views over Borrowdale.

From Grange, detour via the huge boulder known as the Bowder Stone (p91), shifted into position by the long-gone glacier that carved out the Borrowdale Valley. Pootle on to **Rosthwaite** for tea and cake at the **Flock Inn Tea-Room**, or continue to **Seatoller** for lunch.

Honister Pass

From Borrowdale, a narrow, perilously steep road snakes up the fellside to Honister Pass, home to the last working slate mine in the UK. Though you can still pick up slate souvenirs in the on-site shop, these days the Honister Slate Mine (p93) has diversified with a range of adventure activities, ranging from subterranean tours to thrilling via ferrata walks.

Buttermere

Stretching 1.5 miles northwest of Honister Pass, the deep bowl of Buttermere was gouged out by a steamroller glacier, and is backed by a string of impressive peaks and emerald-green hills. The valley's twin lakes, **Buttermere** and **Crummock Water**, were once joined but became separated by glacial silt and rockfall.

The little village of Buttermere sits halfway between the two and provides a wonderfully cosy base for exploring the rest of the valley and the many nearby fells, including **Haystacks** (597m), the favourite mountain and the last resting place of the patron saint of Lakeland walkers, the author Alfred Wainwright (p87).

★ Top Tips

- Buses are a great way to explore Borrowdale and Buttermere.
- If you're planning a return journey the same day, it's nearly always cheaper to buy the **Keswick & Honister Dayrider** (adult/child/family £8.30/6.20/23) than a return fare.

Take a Break

- Buttermere's venerable **Bridge Hotel** (☎017687-70252; www.bridge-hotel.com; mains £10-16; P) offers standard pub food in the bar, or more upmarket fare in the smart-casual restaurant.
- Also in Buttermere village, **Fish Inn** (☎017687-70253; www.fishinnbuttermere.co.uk; mains £8-16; P) once employed the 18th-century beauty known as the 'Maid of Buttermere', but these days it's just a welcoming locals' pub serving basic staples washed down with ales from several local breweries.

Walking Tour

Haystacks

'For a man trying to get a persistent worry out of his mind, the top of Haystacks is a wonderful cure.' So said Alfred Wainwright in Book 7 of his Pictorial Guides, and if anywhere sums up what he loved about the Lakeland fells, it's Haystacks, his favourite mountain. This route follows Wainwright's preferred ascent from Gatesgarth, and descends via the arête of Fleetwith Pike. As always, a map is helpful as the paths can be confusing.

Walk Facts

Start Gatesgarth Farm; 77/77A serves Buttermere and Honister Pass from Keswick

End Gatesgarth Farm

Length 5.5 miles; four to five hours

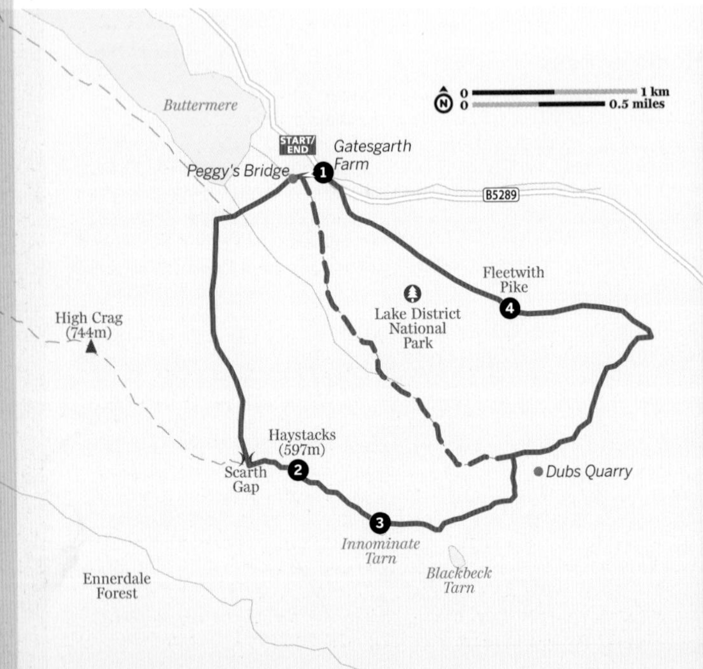

❶ Gatesgarth to Scarth Gap

Park at **Gatesgarth Farm** (or better still, catch the 77 bus from Buttermere). Head southeast across **Peggy's Bridge**, and follow the path as it winds up to the saddle of **Scarth Gap**, a good place for a breather before you tackle the rocky buttress of Haystacks itself.

❷ Haystacks Summit

The climb to the summit is steep but not too testing, although there are a few bits where you'll need hands as well as feet. After 20 minutes or so you'll reach the top of **Haystacks**, with its twin cairns and cluster of little pools. The panorama from the top is grand, stretching northwest across Buttermere, west into Ennerdale and south towards Great Gable.

❸ Innominate Tarn

From here, the path meanders eastwards past two high tarns: **Innominate Tarn**, where Wainwright's ashes were scattered in 1991 as requested in his will, and the reedy pool of **Blackbeck Tarn**. As you descend, you'll pass a left-hand path into Warnscale Bottom, an easy descent if you don't feel like tackling Fleetwith Pike.

❹ Fleetwith Pike

Otherwise, descend towards the slate piles of **Dubs Quarry** and follow the quarry roads before cutting west under Honister Crag. From here, the path leads straight to the summit cairn of **Fleetwith Pike**, with a mind-blowing prospect due west across Buttermere and Crummock Water.

From the top, a clear path leads steeply down the spine of the pike; it's not too difficult, but it is steep and rubbly in places, so take care. Eventually the path levels out onto grassy slopes and descends back to Gatesgarth.

Alfred Wainwright

By far the best-known, best-loved and possibly most-read Lakeland author is the inveterate fell-walker, cartographer and author Alfred Wainwright (or AW to his fans), the man behind the landmark seven-volume guidebook series *The Pictorial Guides to the Lakeland Fells.* Well over half a century after their original publication, Wainwright's guides are still the preferred choice for many fell-walkers, thanks to their hand-illustrated maps, painstaking route descriptions and quirky writing – but most of all, perhaps, for Wainwright's enduring love of the Lakeland landscape, which is apparent on every page. The first guide was published in 1955, and over 60 years later they've sold well over a million copies, making them the bestselling Lake District guidebooks by a long chalk.

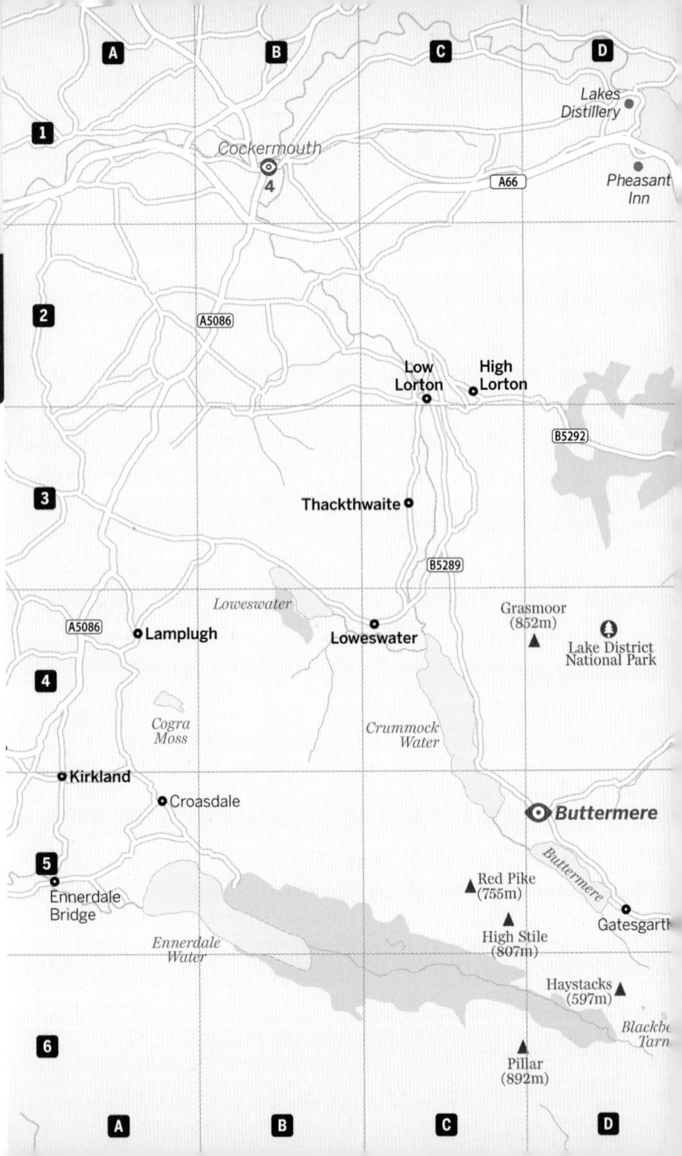

A B C D

1
Lakes Distillery
Cockermouth
4
A66
Pheasant Inn

2
A5086
Low Lorton
High Lorton
B5292

3
Thackthwaite
B5289

4
Loweswater
Grasmoor (852m)
A5086
Lamplugh
Loweswater
Lake District National Park
Cogra Moss
Crummock Water

5
Kirkland
Croasdale
Buttermere
Buttermere
Red Pike (755m)
Ennerdale Bridge
Gatesgarth
High Stile (807m)
Ennerdale Water

6
Haystacks (597m)
Blackbe Tarn
Pillar (892m)

A B C D

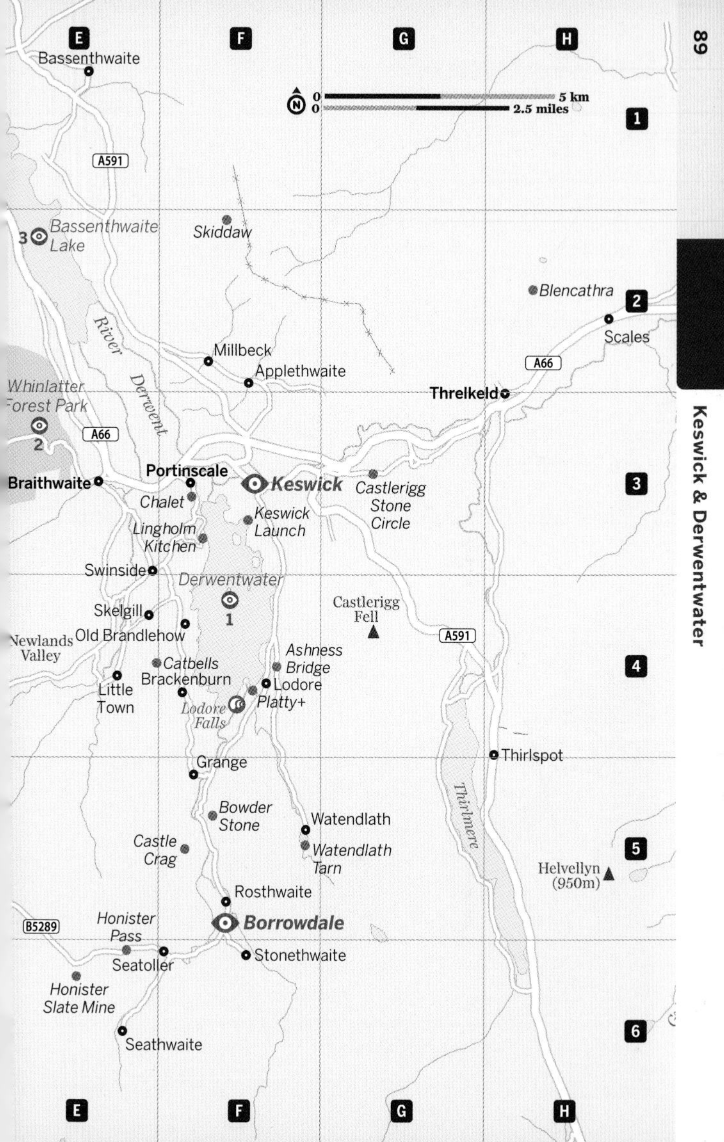

E
F
G
H
1
2
3
4
5
6
0 5 km
0 2.5 miles
Bassenthwaite
A591
Bassenthwaite Lake
3
Skiddaw
Blencathra
Scales
A66
River Derwent
Millbeck
Applethwaite
Threlkeld
Whinlatter Forest Park
2
A66
Braithwaite
Portinscale
Keswick
Castlerigg Stone Circle
Chalet
Keswick Launch
Lingholm Kitchen
Swinside
Derwentwater
1
Castlerigg Fell
Skelgill
Newlands Valley
Old Brandlehow
A591
Ashness Bridge
Catbells
Brackenburn
Lodore
Little Town
Lodore Falls
Platty+
Thirlspot
Grange
Thirlmere
Bowder Stone
Watendlath
Watendlath Tarn
Castle Crag
Helvellyn (950m)
Rosthwaite
Honister Pass
B5289
Borrowdale
Seatoller
Stonethwaite
Honister Slate Mine
Seathwaite

Derwentwater

1 MAP P88, F4

Shimmering to the south of Keswick, studded with islands and ringed by craggy fells, Derwentwater is undoubtedly one of the prettiest of the Lakeland lakes.

As always, getting out on the water is the best way to explore. The **Keswick Launch** (017687-72263; www.keswick-launch.co.uk; round-the-lake pass adult/child/family £10.75/5.65/25.50) runs regular cross-lake excursions, and rowing boats and motor boats (£12/27 per hour) can be hired next to the jetties.

It's a little out of the way, in Portinscale, but cafe **Chalet** (017687-72757; www.thechaletportinscale.co.uk; lunch £3.50-8.95; 9am-5pm) is a popular stop-off for passengers on the Keswick Launch, with a lunch menu of flatbreads, stone-baked pizzas and deli boards served on a piece of local slate. Stacked-up logs and wooden furniture give it a Scandinavian vibe.

Nearby is the splendid cafe **Lingholm Kitchen** (017687-71206; www.thelingholmkitchen.co.uk; mains £7-9; 9am-5pm), set in a delightful walled garden on the Lingholme Estate, with a 30m glass wall that presents cinematic views of Skiddaw, plus a dainty old greenhouse. For lunch, expect modern brunch dishes such as chickpea fritters, baked eggs, pork croquettes and (of course) avocado on toast.

Bowder Stone

Hiking near Keswick & Derwentwater

There are some awesome fells within easy reach of Keswick, and near Derwentwater:

- The mini-mountain of **Catbells** (451m) packs a punch considering its modest height. The classic path starts near the Hawse End jetty on Derwentwater's west side, from where the path rises steeply for around 1.5 miles to the summit, with sweeping views over Skiddaw, the Newlands Valley and Borrowdale. The best way to the jetty is aboard the Keswick Launch.

- Sometimes known by its alternative name of Saddleback, **Blencathra** (868m) looms along the skyline northeast of Keswick, and (alongside Skiddaw) represents the toughest hiking challenge in the area. The usual route starts in Threlkeld and loops around the fell's east side over **Blease Fell**, a steep climb that's well worthwhile for the panoramic view. It's about 5 miles return.

- One of only four Lakeland fells above 915m (3000ft), the great hump of **Skiddaw** (931m) dominates Keswick's northern skyline. It's a long, steep and tiring puff to the top (slog is a fairly common description), but on a clear day the mountain's panorama more than matches the other three highest peaks. It's 8 miles return, or around five hours of walking.

- Once a slate mine, the scree-strewn hillock of **Castle Crag** (985m) provides knockout views across Borrowdale. It's reached along a mainly level trail from Grange, but it gets steep towards the end and the heaps of slate on the hillside make the going slippery in the wet. There are several side junctions on the way; bring a map to avoid getting lost.

Other natural features in the area worth visiting:

- National Trust–owned **Watendlath Tarn** is reached via a turn-off on the B5285 south of Keswick. On the way the road passes over one of the Lake District's most photographed packhorse crossings at **Ashness Bridge**. Parking at the tarn is free for NT members, but the road is narrow and has few passing places, so it's more pleasant to walk up in summer.

- A mile south from Grange, a turn-off leads up to the geological curiosity known as the **Bowder Stone**, a 1700-tonne lump of rock left behind by a retreating glacier. A small stepladder leads to the top of the rock.

Newlands Valley

Comparatively few people make the trek to the Newlands Valley, the hidden valley that runs southwest for 7 miles from the village of Braithwaite, just west of Keswick, all the way to Buttermere, climbing over the high point of Newlands Hause (333m) en route.

It's a wild and almost completely empty landscape, only interrupted by a handful of remote farms and cottages, so it's ideal hiking country. The classic circuit is the 9- to 10-mile **Newlands Horseshoe**, which runs from the tiny village of Little Town and over the tops of Robinson, Hindscarth, Dalehead, High Spy and Maiden Moor.

At the southern end of Derwentwater are the famous **Lodore Falls** waterfall featured in a poem by Robert Southey, but it's only worth visiting after a good spell of rain. It's in the grounds of the Lodore Hotel; there's an honesty box for donations.

Based near the falls at the Lodore Boat Landings, **Platty+** (017687-76572; www.plattyplus.co.uk; kayaks & canoes per hour £8-15) hires out kayaks, canoes, rowing boats and sailing dinghies. It also runs instruction courses.

Whinlatter Forest Park

2 MAP P88, E3

Encompassing 4.6 sq miles of pine, larch and spruce, **Whinlatter Forest Park** (www.forestry.gov.uk/whinlatter; free) is England's only true mountain forest, rising sharply to 790m about 5 miles from Keswick. The forest is a designated red squirrel reserve; you can check out live video feeds from squirrel cams at the **visitor centre** (017687-78469; 10am-4pm). It's also home to two exciting mountain-bike trails and the **Go Ape** (www.goape.co.uk/days-out/whinlatter; adult/child £33/25; 9am-5pm mid-Mar–Oct) treetop assault course. You can hire bikes from **Cyclewise** (017687-78711; www.cyclewise.co.uk; 3hr hire adult/child from £19.50/15; 10am-5pm), next to the visitor centre.

For a secluded spot to eat or stay, head for out-of-the-way bolthole **Cottage in the Wood** (017687-78409; www.thecottageinthewood.co.uk; Braithwaite; set menu £45; restaurant 6.30-9pm Tue-Sat; P), on the road to Whinlatter Forest, in a completely modernised coaching inn. The restaurant's fantastic, while elegant rooms (d £130-220) survey woods and countryside: the Mountain View rooms overlook the Skiddaw Range, but we liked the superprivate Attic

Suite and the Garden Room, with its wood floors and wet room.

Bassenthwaite Lake

3 MAP P88, E2

Three miles north of Keswick, Bassenthwaite is one of the few lakes undisturbed by cruise boats and pleasure vessels. Much of the shoreline is privately owned, but there are options for a drink and a meal.

The first craft distillery in the Lake District, **Lakes Distillery** (017687-88850; www.lakesdistillery.com; tours £12.50; 11am-6pm) has made a big splash since opening in 2014. It's located on a 'model farm' built during the 1850s and was founded by a team of master distillers. So far its range includes a gin, a vodka and a flagship whisky, plus liqueurs flavoured with damson plum, elderflower, rhubarb and rosehip, and salted caramel. Guided tours take you through the process and include a tasting of the three spirits.

You can also take a specialist whisky tour, and meet the resident herd of alpacas. The **Bistro at the Distillery** (mains £14–30) is worth a look for lunch too.

A short drive along Bassen thwaite Lake is fine-dining pub **Pheasant Inn** (017687-76234; www.the-pheasant.co.uk; mains £13.50-21, restaurant dinner menu £45; restaurant 7-9pm Wed-Sat, noon-2.30pm Sun, bistro noon-2.30pm & 6-9pm). Hunting prints and pewter tankards cover the old bar, stocked with vintage whiskies and Lakeland ales, and the two restaurants (informal bistro and very formal restaurant) serve superior country food. The afternoon tea's done in the proper English fashion too, served on a tiered cake stand with scones and cucumber sandwiches.

Honister Slate Mine

The old **Honister Slate Mine** (Map p88; 017687-77230; www.honister.com; mine tour adult/child £14.50/8.50, all-day pass incl mine tour & classic/extreme via ferrata £56.50/64; tours 10.30am, 12.30pm & 3.30pm Mar-Oct) has been reinvented as a centre for all kinds of activities: you could venture underground into the bowels of the old 'Edge' and 'Kimberley' mines, tackle a **via ferrata** (classic route £40, extreme incl Infinity Bridge £45, all-day pass incl mine tour & classic/extreme via ferrata £56.50/64), or climb inside the mine along a system of fixed cables, tracing the route followed by the slate miners. A tour into the 'Cathedral' mine runs on Friday by request, but you'll need eight people and it costs £25 per person. The mine is at Honister Pass (p85).

Cockermouth

4 MAP P88, B1

The poet William Wordsworth was born on 7 April 1770 at handsome Georgian **Wordsworth House** (NT; 01900-824805; www.nationaltrust.org.uk/wordsworth-house; Main St; adult/child £7.90/3.95; 11am-5pm Sat-Thu Mar-Oct). Built around 1745, the house has been meticulously restored based on accounts from the Wordsworth archive: the kitchen, drawing room, study and bedrooms all look much as they would have to a young William. Costumed guides wander around the house for added period authenticity. Outside, the walled kitchen garden was mentioned in Wordsworth's autobiographical epic *The Prelude*.

There are numerous dining and drinking options in Cockermouth.

On aptly named Brewery Lane, you'll find **Jennings Brewery** (01900-821011; www.jenningsbrewery.co.uk; adult/child £9/4.50; guided tours 1.30pm Wed-Sat). Real-ale aficionados will be familiar with the Jennings name – it has been brewing beers since 1874 and its pints are pulled at pubs all over the Lake District. Guided tours trace the brewing process, followed by a tasting session of Cocker Hoop and Sneck Lifter in the Old Cooperage Bar. Children must be over 12.

Whitewashed **Trout Hotel** (01900-823591; www.trouthotel.co.uk; Crown St; 2-/3-course dinner menu £21.95/24.95; P) has been a feature in Cockermouth since

Castlerigg stone circle

Castlerigg Stone Circle

Of all the Lake District's stone circles, none has the drama of **Castlerigg** (Map p88; free), perched on a lonely hilltop a mile above Keswick. Constructed between 3000 and 4000 years ago, the circle contains between 38 and 42 stones (depending on which ones you count), with a further rectangle of stones set inside the main ring; the tallest is around 8ft high, and the largest weighs over 16 tonnes.

Quite how the ancient Britons dragged these massive lumps of rock to this isolated spot remains a mystery, and archaeologists are still divided over its purpose – some think it's a prehistoric market place or monument, while others believe it's a celestial calendar that marked the passing seasons. The circle is signposted off the A66 and A591.

the late 17th century, and has heritage in spades (it was a favourite of Bing Crosby, who liked to fish nearby). There's a choice of dining settings: the informal Terrace Bistro and the more sophisticated Derwent Restaurant, where you can dine on seared scallops, pork belly and bubble-and-squeak risotto.

Even if you're a committed carnivore, it's well worth dining at **Quince & Medlar** (☎01900-823579; www.quinceandmedlar.co.uk; 13 Castlegate; mains £15.50; ⏲7-10pm Tue-Sat; 🌶) to see that vegetarian food isn't just nut roast and baked mushrooms – here, you could find yourself feasting on courgette-wrapped cheese soufflé, root veg and puy lentil 'haggis' or French-onion tartlet. The location in a Georgian house is very handsome.

Cockermouth fave **Merienda** (☎017687-72024; www.merienda.co.uk; 7a Station St; mains £4-8; ⏲8am-9pm Mon-Thu, to 10pm Fri & Sat, 9am-9pm Sun) is open daily and has a second branch in Keswick. The interior is light and airy and the Med-tinged food is packed with flavour. There's a good balance between meat and veggie-friendly dishes. Carnivores might enjoy a generous slow-cooked BBQ brisket burger, while herbivores should try the excellent baked eggs with feta and aubergine.

Bitter End (☎01900-828993; www.bitterend.co.uk; 15 Kirkgate; ⏲noon-2.30pm & 6-10pm) brewpub produces its own award-winning beers such as Cockermouth Pride, Lakeland Honey Beer and Cuddy Lugs. You can watch the vats at work through a glass partition in the bar.

Explore

Ullswater

After Windermere, the second-largest lake in the Lake District is Ullswater, stretching for 7.5 miles between Pooley Bridge at the northern end and Glenridding and Patterdale at the southern end. Carved out by a long-extinct glacier, the deep valley in which the lake sits is flanked by an impressive string of fells, most notably the razor ridge of Helvellyn (p100), Cumbria's third-highest mountain at 950m.

Begin the day in Pooley Bridge with breakfast at Granny Dowbekin's (p103), then hop on board the Ullswater 'Steamers' (p103) for a cruise along Ullswater. Alight at Howtown and walk up Hallin Fell (p107) for impressive views. Get back on the boat and cruise to Glenridding, having a late lunch at Fellbites (p106). Spend the afternoon wandering through Gowbarrow Park (p98) to the waterfall at Aira Force. If your legs are up to it, you could even head up Gowbarrow Fell (p99) for sunset. For dinner, head for 1863 (p104) in Pooley Bridge.

Getting There & Around

Bus 508 travels from Penrith to Glenridding and Patterdale. Five buses continue over Kirkstone Pass to Windermere.

The winding A592 runs along Ullswater's west shore, linking Pooley Bridge, Glenridding and Patterdale; a minor road runs along the east side to Howtown and Martindale.

Ullswater Map on p102

Mute swan, Ullswater

Top Sights

Gowbarrow Park & Aira Force

This expansive park on the west shore of Ullswater is one of the best-known beauty spots in the eastern Lakes – famously, it was one of Wordsworth's favourite places for a walk, and is celebrated for its springtime displays of daffodils. It's also home to a brace of impressive waterfalls.

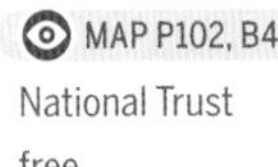

MAP P102, B4

National Trust

free

The Path to Aira Force

Southwest of Pooley Bridge, the A592 ducks and dives along Ullswater's western shore. After five miles you'll reach the small National Trust car park at Gowbarrow Park, founded by the Howard family (owners of nearby Greystoke Castle) as a hunting park and leisure garden, but now run by the National Trust.

The car park marks the start of the half-hour stroll to Aira Force, one of the most famous waterfalls in the Lake District. The 20m cascade makes for a furious sight after heavy rain, with its clashing waters tumbling down into a densely wooded ravine lined with spruce, fir, pine and cedar. Red squirrels are frequent visitors to the woods around the falls, so keep your eyes peeled.

If the inevitable crowds around the falls are a little too much, you can continue your walk along the wooded trail to **High Force**, or strike out for the summit of **Gowbarrow Fell** (pictured; 481m).

Glencoyne Bay

Just south of Gowbarrow Park is the little inlet of Glencoyne Bay, famous as the inspiration for one of Wordsworth's poems. During a springtime walk on 15 April 1802, Dorothy and William stumbled across a sprightly stand of daffodils swaying in the breeze, a sight which may have inspired the most quoted lines in English poetry: 'I wandered lonely as a cloud...'

Needless to say, springtime is the best time to visit if you want to see the blooms, but do resist the urge to pick them – unless you fancy a slap on the wrist from a National Park Authority warden.

★ Top Tips

- The main car park at Gowbarrow Park is very expensive and is often full in summer – but if you're a National Trust member, you get to park for free.
- Arrive early or late to avoid the crowds.

Take a Break

There is a small National Trust cafe near the main car park.

Walking Tour

Helvellyn

Next to Scafell Pike, the Lake District's second-most popular mountain is Helvellyn, especially the classic ridge route along Striding Edge. It's busy year-round, but it's a challenge even for experienced walkers, with dizzying drops and some all-fours scrambling. It's best avoided if you're wary of heights, and don't even think about it in wintry conditions – but there are few Lakeland walks that feel more rewarding.

Walk Facts

Start Patterdale; 508 travels from Penrith to Patterdale, some services continue to Windermere

End Patterdale

Length 8 miles, six to seven hours

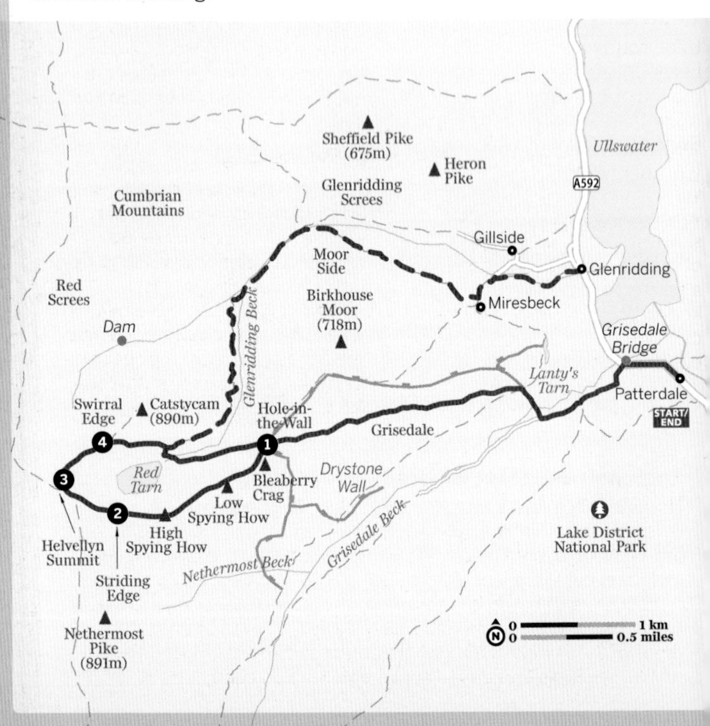

❶ Patterdale to the Hole-in-the-Wall

There are several possible routes to the top of Helvellyn. This one heads west from Patterdale. After about half a mile, cross Grisedale Beck via a humpback bridge before ascending the flank of Birkhouse Moor. After a long, steep climb you'll reach the **Hole-in-the-Wall**, a good place to take a breather, with views up to the Helvellyn summit, Red Tarn and the ragged spine of Striding Edge.

❷ Striding Edge

Head southwest beneath Bleaberry Crag and over the rocky mound of High Spying How. Then it's onto the ridge of **Striding Edge** itself. Several trails wind their way along the edge, offering various degrees of difficulty; whichever you choose, walk slowly and carefully. At the end of the ridge there's the option of a scramble over the rock tower known as the Chimney, or you can avoid it by following along an easier path on the right.

❸ Helvellyn Summit

From here, another sharp, rocky section leads to **Helvellyn summit** (950m). The views are truly fabulous: southeast to St Sunday Crag, northeast to the pointy peak of Catstycam, west to Thirlmere and east to Ullswater.

Three memorials can be found around the summit: the first to Robert Dixon, who slipped off the peak while following a foxhound's trail, and a second to the climber Charles Gough who, in 1805, became the first recorded person to fall off the mountain. A third memorial marks the point where two daring pilots, John Leeming and Bert Hinkler, landed their plane on 22 December 1926.

❹ Swirral Edge

Descend via **Swirral Edge**, following the path between Catstycam and Red Tarn. It's nearly as dramatic as its sister ridge on Striding Edge. Both are classic glacial ridges, formed by the movement of glaciers during the last ice age. You can now retrace your steps back to Patterdale or follow the path along Red Tarn Beck to Glenridding.

England's Hardiest Hikers

On your walk, spare a thought for the Helvellyn Weatherline Assessors, employed by the national park to climb the mountain every day between December and March to assess the risk of avalanches and routine weather conditions such as wind chill, snow depth and temperature. This info is recorded on the Lake District Weatherline (www.lakedistrictweatherline.co.uk), a service relied upon by hundreds of thousands of hill walkers every year. The Assessors also run Winter Skills Courses to educate walkers on hiking safety.

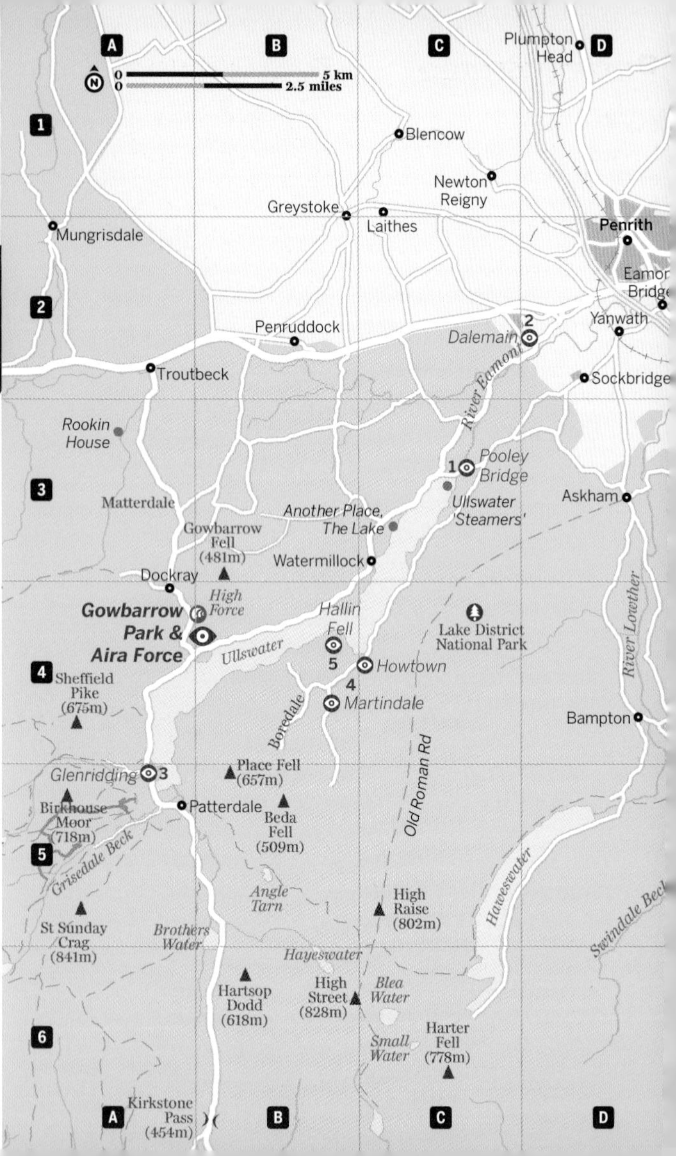

A
B
C
D
0 5 km
0 2.5 miles
1
2
3
4
5
6

Plumpton Head
Blencow
Newton Reigny
Greystoke
Laithes
Penrith
Eamont Bridge
Mungrisdale
Penruddock
Yanwath
2 Dalemain
Troutbeck
Sockbridge
River Eamont
Rookin House
1 Pooley Bridge
Ullswater 'Steamers'
Askham
Matterdale
Another Place, The Lake
Gowbarrow Fell (481m)
Watermillock
Dockray
High Force
Gowbarrow Park & Aira Force
Hallin Fell
Lake District National Park
Ullswater
5
Howtown
4
Martindale
River Lowther
Sheffield Pike (675m)
Boredale
Bampton
Old Roman Rd
Place Fell (657m)
Glenridding 3
Birkhouse Moor (718m)
Patterdale
Beda Fell (509m)
Grisedale Beck
Angle Tarn
High Raise (802m)
Haweswater
Swindale Beck
St Sunday Crag (841m)
Brothers Water
Hayeswater
Hartsop Dodd (618m)
High Street (828m)
Blea Water
Small Water
Harter Fell (778m)
Kirkstone Pass (454m)
A
B
C
D

Pooley Bridge

1 MAP P102, C3

Nestled at the head of the lake alongside the babbling River Eamont, the tiny hamlet of Pooley Bridge is little more than a gaggle of pubs, cottages and teashops. The main reason to stop here is to climb aboard **Ullswater's 'Steamers'** (017684-82229; www.ullswater-steamers.co.uk; cruise all piers pass adult/child £15.95/6.95), a memorable way to explore the lake. The various vessels include the stately *Lady of the Lake*, launched in 1877 and supposedly the world's oldest working passenger boat. The boats run east–west from Pooley Bridge to Glenridding via Howtown; there are nine daily sailings in summer, three in winter.

A single fare from Pooley Bridge to Glenridding is adult/child £9.85/5.90, so it's better value to buy the 'all piers' pass, which stays valid for 24 hours and also gets you 50% off fares on the Ravenglass & Eskdale Railway (p118). If you're walking the **Ullswater Way** (www.ullswaterway.co.uk), you can also buy a five-day walker's ticket (£41.60/21.95).

For a filling all-day brekkie, a ploughman's lunch, chunky sandwich or a slice of something naughty and cake-shaped, **Granny Dowbekin's** (017684-86453; www.grannydowbekins.co.uk; mains £6-12; 9am-5pm) is a favourite option. The homemade 'gingerbridge' makes a yummy souvenir.

Striding Edge, Helvellyn (p100)

Luxe by the Lake

Acquired by the owners of Cornwall's Watergate Bay Hotel, the former Rampsbeck Hotel has been reinvented as one of the Lakes' most luxurious, family-friendly, activity-focused getaways, **Another Place, The Lake** (Map p102; 017684-86442; www.another.place; Watermillock; 4-course meal £40; P). The Rampsbeck restaurant is excellent. There is also a bar, well-stocked library and lakefront lawns, and activities including stand-up paddleboarding, kayaking and wild swimming. A new wing has added an infinity pool and contemporary rooms (r £230–£290, f £345–£385); rooms in the old house feel more traditional.

A classy new addition to Pooley Bridge's dining scene is **1863** (017684-86334; www.1863ullswater.co.uk; High St; mains £13.50-22.50; dinner 6-9pm, bar 2-10pm), overseen by head chef Phil Corrie, who has a fondness for the classics but is abreast of modern tastes too – so you get dishes like Goosnargh Chicken with morels and truffled potato, or mead-glazed duck with sweet damson jam.

Rookin House

Ever fancied driving a JCB or an Argocat? Now's your chance! **Rookin House** (Map p102; 017684-83561; www.rookinhouse.co.uk), between Penrith and Keswick, offers a huge range of outdoor fun, from the usual horse riding, clay-pigeon shooting and archery to the weird and wonderful.

Dalemain

2 MAP P102, D2

Driving southwest along the A592 road from Penrith, you can't miss the striking salmon-pink facade of **Dalemain** (017684-86450; www.dalemain.com; house & gardens adult/child £11.75/free, gardens only £8.75/free; house 10.30am-3.30pm, gardens 10am-4.30pm Sun-Thu), a mile from Ullswater's northern tip. With a name deriving from the Old Norse for 'manor in the valley', this elegant country estate traces its roots back to the reign of Henry II. Inside it's the picture of an English country house – half *Gosford Park* set, half three-dimensional Cluedo board, with a bewildering maze of passages, spiralling staircases and interconnecting rooms.

Although the Georgian facade was constructed during the mid-18th century, behind its orderly frontage are the remnants of a 12th-century pele tower and an Elizabethan manor. Since 1679 the house has been owned by the Hasell dynasty. Family photos and heirlooms are dotted around amongst the antiques, Chippendale furniture and priceless oil portraits. Highlights include the Chinese Room with its handmade oriental wallpaper; the Tudor Fretwork Room, with its oak panelling and ornate plaster ceiling; and the fascinating servants' quarters. Tea is served in the medieval Great Hall. Outside, the grounds feature a Tudor knot garden and a wonderful rose walk. The 16th-century Great Barn houses two small agricultural museums, while in the base of the Norman pele tower is a museum dedicated to the Westmorland and Cumberland Yeomanry regiment, founded in 1819 and disbanded shortly after WWI. The house hosts lots of festivals and events throughout the year, including country shows, tractor meets, classic car displays and a thoroughly British **Marmalade Festival**, held in March. The **Mansions, Boots & Boats Ticket** (adult/child £20/7.90) also includes an all-day pass aboard Ullswater 'Steamers'. It can only be purchased online through the Dalemain website.

Glenridding

3 MAP P102, A5

At the southern end of Ullswater is the tiny hamlet of Glenridding, home to the **Glenridding Sailing Centre** (☎017684-82541; www.glenriddingsailingcentre.co.uk), the

St Martin's (p106)

KEVIN EAVES / SHUTTERSTOCK ©

lake's main sailing centre, which hires out canoes (£15/40 for one/three hours), kayaks (£10/25 for one/three hours) and a range of sailboats and dinghies (£70 to £110 per day). It also offers RSA sailing courses.

When you're done boating and hunger strikes, **Fellbites** (☎017684-82781; lunch mains £3.95-9.95, dinner mains £12.50-18; ⏰9am-8.30pm Thu-Tue, to 5.30pm Wed), next to the main car park in Glenridding, has something to fill you up at any time of day: generous fry-ups for breakfast; soups, pulled-pork burgers and rarebits (a kind of sophisticated cheese on toast, generously drizzled with a secret ingredient tasting suspiciously like beer) for lunch; lamb shanks and duck breast for dinner. It's honest, no-fuss grub.

For pub food and a pint with a view of the fells, try **Traveller's Rest** (☎017684-82298; Glenridding; mains £5.50-15; ⏰10am-11pm), a Glenridding stalwart. The food might be plain (steaks, pies, mixed grills) but the portions are huge.

Howtown & Martindale

4 MAP P102, C4 & B4

Ullswater's west side gets busy, but few people take the time to explore the lake's eastern side. The little hamlet of Howtown is perfect for an expedition into the nearby peaks, either an ascent of Hallin Fell (p105), or the more challenging charge along the old Roman road of High Street. It's worth venturing on to see the little church of **St Martin's**, overlooking the remote Martindale valley.

Sheltered under the boughs of a thousand-year-old yew, the church has a flagstoned interior housing a 17th-century pulpit and a 500-year-old church bell.It's worth noting that the narrow, twisty road

Haweswater

The most easterly of the Lake District's waters, Haweswater is also one of its most remote – it can only be reached via a narrow, winding road that feels at times like you're heading off the edge of the map. In fact, it's not actually a lake but a reservoir created in 1935. Sometimes during exceptionally dry spells, the remains of the drowned village of Mardale appear above the waterline. It's a great area to escape the hiking crowds and is popular with wildlife-spotters too – sometimes golden eagles can be seen soaring over the fells.

Kirkstone Pass

South of Ullswater the main A592 climbs past the modest splashes of Brothers Water and Hayeswater en route to Kirkstone Pass – at 454m the highest mountain pass in Cumbria open to road traffic.

It's one of the most scenic stretches of road in the whole national park, but it's not always easy going: the upper section as you pass the whitewashed Kirkstone Pass Inn (www.kirkstonepassinn.com) is rather ominously known as the 'Struggle'. Every winter unsuspecting drivers are caught out by surprise patches of black ice and snow, only to find themselves coming to an abrupt stop against a drystone wall.

winding along the lake's eastern edge to Howtown is best avoided if you're a bad reverser – it's single-track pretty much the whole way from Pooley Bridge, and passing places are few and far between. A better way to arrive is via the Ullswater Steamers (p103), which call in at the Howtown jetty en route from Glenridding and Pooley Bridge.

Hallin Fell

5 MAP P102, B4

For a quick up-and-down jaunt, this little 388m-high fell on Ullswater's east side is hard to beat: though it's one of the smallest, the knockout views from the top are quite out of proportion to its diminutive size. The easiest way up is to catch an Ullswater Steamer to Howtown and follow the trail towards Martindale Church and the summit.

Explore

Western Lakes & Cumbrian Coast

The western Lakes is where the landscape takes a turn for the wild. The main draw here is the valley of Wasdale, home to England's highest mountain (Scafell Pike) and deepest lake (Wastwater). Further west, Cumbria's underappreciated coastline is well worth exploring too.

Start with a wander around the old port of Whitehaven and a walk to St Bees Head (p116) for seabird-spotting. Then it's a dramatic drive into Wasdale to glimpse Scafell Pike (p112), followed by lunch at the Wasdale Head Inn (p117). After lunch, continue south to Ravenglass for a ride on the Ravenglass & Eskdale Railway (p118), or alternatively a visit to Holker Hall (p110). Either way, end up in Cartmel for supper at one of experimental chef Simon Rogan's restaurants: L'Enclume (p122) or Rogan & Company (p122).

Getting There & Around

Having a car really helps here, as there is no public transport to Wasdale. The main A595 runs along the coast; to get to Wasdale, you need to turn off near Gosforth, following signs to Nether Wasdale.

The Furness and Cumbrian Coast railway lines loop 120 miles from Lancaster to Carlisle, stopping at the coastal resorts of Grange, Ulverston, Ravenglass, Whitehaven and Workington. The Cumbria Coast Day Ranger (adult/child £20.20/10.10) covers a day's unlimited travel on the line.

Western Lakes & Cumbrian Coast Map on p114

Wasdale (p117) from Great Gable

Top Sights

Holker Hall

If you're looking for Cumbria's answer to Downton Abbey, you'll find it at Holker Hall. Three miles east of Cartmel on the B5278, this has been the family seat of the Cavendish family for nigh on four centuries, and it's a classic example of English aristocratic architecture.

MAP P114, F7

015395-58328

www.holker.co.uk

adult/child £12.50/free

house 11am-4pm, grounds 10.30am-5pm Wed-Sun Mar-Oct

History

Though parts of the house (pictured) date from the 16th century, it was almost entirely rebuilt following a devastating fire in 1871. It's a typically ostentatious Victorian affair, covered with mullioned windows, gables and copper-topped turrets outside and filled with a warren of lavishly over-the-top rooms inside.

The Long Gallery

The showstopper room is the incredible Long Gallery, notable for its plasterwork ceiling and fine English furniture – look for the 19th-century sphinx-legged table and a wonderful walnut cabinet inlaid with ivory and rosewood.

The Drawing Room & Library

The drawing room is an equally impressive affair, packed with Chippendale furniture and historic oil paintings of family notables. Nearby, the library contains an antique microscope belonging to Henry Cavendish (discoverer of nitric acid) and more than 3500 antique books (some of which are fakes, designed to conceal light switches when the house was converted to electric power in 1911).

The Gardens

Outside, Holker's wonderful grounds sprawl for more than 10 hectares, encompassing a rose garden, a woodland, ornamental fountains and a 22m-high lime tree (said to be one of the largest in England).

There's also a superb **food hall** that stocks produce from the estate, including two renowned products: venison and salt-marsh lamb. The tidal grasses are said to give the lamb a distinctive salty flavour.

★ Top Tips

- You'll need at least two hours to visit the house, or more if you would like to explore the grounds as well.
- If you only wish to explore the gardens, there is a £4 discount on admission.
- Children up to 16 years old visit free of charge.

Take a Break

Light lunches are available in the **Courtyard Cafe** (meals £4.95-9.95; open 10.30am-5pm daily;), while more sophisticated fare is served at the **Ilex Bar & Brasserie** (mains £10-14; open noon-3pm Wed-Sun).

Walking Tour

Scafell Pike

Every year thousands of hikers set out to conquer England's highest mountain and, despite its 978m height, it's achievable as long as you're fit, equipped and prepared for a slog. The exposed summit and altitude make this walk dangerous and difficult to navigate during bad weather. Proper supplies, compass and map are essential whatever the weather. Stick to the path wherever possible, as trail erosion is becoming a big problem on Scafell Pike.

Walk Facts

Start Wasdale Head

End Wasdale Head

Length 7 miles; six hours

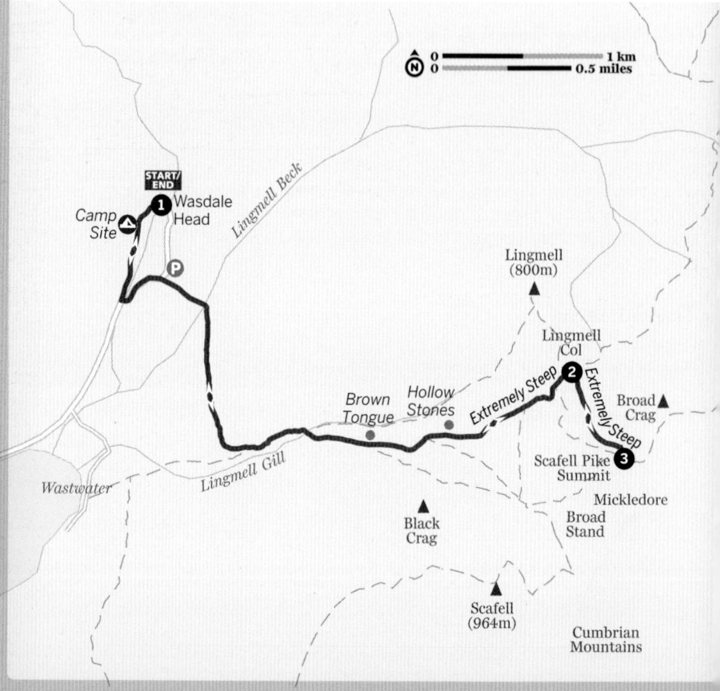

❶ Wasdale Head to Brown Tongue

There are several routes to the top, but this classic ascent starts from the **Wasdale Head** car park. Head south over Lingmell Beck and follow the path up towards **Lingmell Gill**. Cross the stones over the beck and continue climbing steeply up the track along **Brown Tongue**, overlooked to the south by the stern cliffs of Black and Scafell crags. Take a breather here.

❷ Lingmell Col

You'll soon reach a junction: the right fork leads to an alternative ascent of the peak via the scree-covered pass of Mickledore. Take the left fork instead, traversing the boulder-strewn expanse of **Hollow Stones** onto a long zigzagging trail up to **Lingmell Col**, where the route ascends southeast over a shattered plain of rocks, scree and boulders all the way up to the highest point in England.

❸ Scafell Pike Summit

A large cairn marks the actual **summit** (978m). You almost certainly won't be alone: even on the worst days, someone seems to set out to conquer the mountain, and on sunny summer days it can be uncomfortably crowded. The views across the valley are astounding, especially the interlocking panorama of peaks to the north, including Great Gable, Kirk Fell, Green Gable and Pillar. Scafell looms to the southwest, across the narrow ridge of Mickledore; look out for rock climbers tackling the classic challenge of Broad Stand nearby.

Once you've basked in the views, retrace your steps from the summit plateau all the way back down to **Wasdale Head**. Pat yourself on the back – you've just conquered the nation's loftiest hiking challenge.

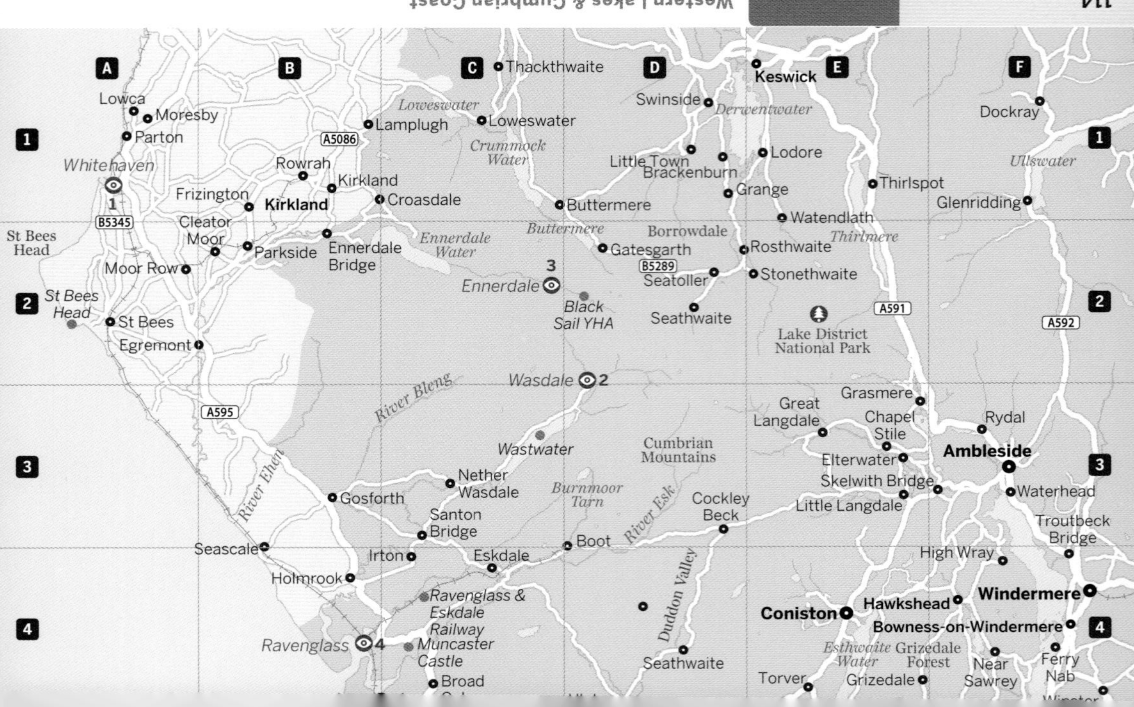
A
B
C
D
E
F
1
2
3
4
Lowca
Moresby
Parton
Whitehaven
1
B5345
St Bees Head
St Bees Head
St Bees
Egremont
Moor Row
Cleator Moor
Frizington
Kirkland
Rowrah
Kirkland
Parkside
Ennerdale Bridge
Croasdale
Lamplugh
A5086
Loweswater
Loweswater
Crummock Water
Thackthwaite
Ennerdale Water
Buttermere
Buttermere
3
Ennerdale
Black Sail YHA
Gatesgarth
B5289
Seatoller
Seathwaite
Borrowdale
Swinside
Derwentwater
Little Town
Brackenburn
Grange
Lodore
Keswick
Watendlath
Rosthwaite
Stonethwaite
Thirlmere
Thirlspot
A591
Lake District National Park
Dockray
Ullswater
Glenridding
A592
River Bleng
Wasdale
2
A595
Wastwater
River Ehen
Gosforth
Nether Wasdale
Santon Bridge
Burnmoor Tarn
Cumbrian Mountains
River Esk
Seascale
Irton
Eskdale
Boot
Holmrook
Ravenglass & Eskdale Railway
Ravenglass
4
Muncaster Castle
Broad
Duddon Valley
Seathwaite
Cockley Beck
Grasmere
Great Langdale
Chapel Stile
Elterwater
Skelwith Bridge
Little Langdale
Rydal
Ambleside
Waterhead
Troutbeck Bridge
High Wray
Windermere
Hawkshead
Coniston
Bowness-on-Windermere
Esthwaite Water
Grizedale Forest
Grizedale
Torver
Near Sawrey
Ferry Nab

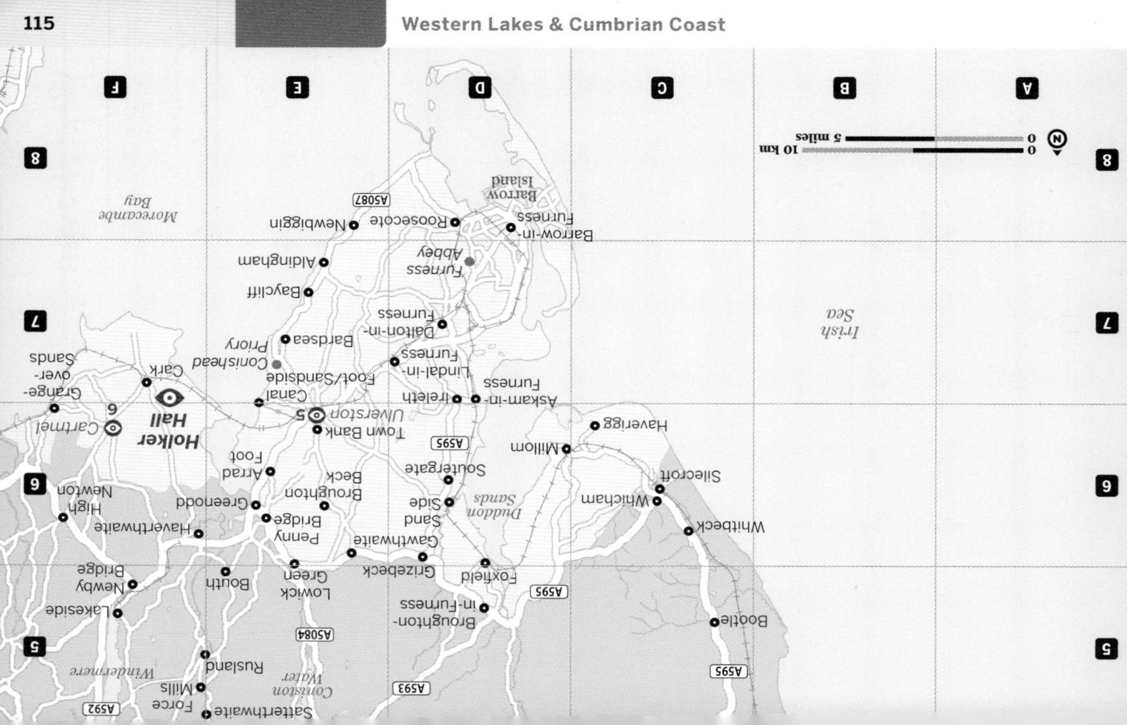
A
B
C
D
E
F
5
6
7
8
0
0
5 miles
10 km
Irish Sea
Morecambe Bay
Windermere
Coniston Water
Duddon Sands
A592
A593
A5084
A595
A5087
Satterthwaite
Force Mills
Rusland
Lakeside
Newby Bridge
Bouth
Lowick Green
Broughton-in-Furness
Bootle
Foxfield
Grizebeck
Gawthwaite
Penny Bridge
Haverthwaite
High Newton
Greenodd
Broughton Beck
Sand Side
Whitbeck
Whicham
Silecroft
Soutergate
Arrad Foot
Millom
Haverigg
Holker Hall
Cartmel
6
Town Bank
Ulverston
5
Grange-over-Sands
Canal Foot/Sandside
Cark
Ireleth
Askam-in-Furness
Lindal-in-Furness
Conishead Priory
Bardsea
Dalton-in-Furness
Baycliff
Furness Abbey
Aldingham
Barrow-in-Furness
Roosecote
Newbiggin
Barrow Island

Whitehaven

1 MAP 114, A1

In the coastal town of Whitehaven, **Beacon** (01946-592302; www.thebeacon-whitehaven.co.uk; West Strand; adult/child £5.50/2; 10am-4.30pm Tue-Sun) is an intriguing museum that explores the town's maritime history. It's split into four levels: floor 1 hosts temporary exhibitions; floor 2 explores the history of the nuclear plant at Sellafield; and floor 3 explores the history of the Copeland area, from Roman archaeology to Whitehaven's maritime trade. On the top floor you can look through telescopes and explore the science of maps and weather forecasting. It's geared towards kids, but it's quite informative.

Find out all about Whitehaven's rum-running history through a mix of waxwork models and dioramas at **Rum Story** (01946-592933; www.rumstory.co.uk; Lowther St; adult/child £5.95/3.95; 10am-4.30pm Easter-Sep, 10am-4.30pm Mon-Sat Oct-Easter;), a budget museum that includes an 18th-century sugar workshop and a debauched 'punch tavern'. It's fun, if tacky.

Five-and-a-half miles south of Whitehaven and 1½ miles north of the tiny town of St Bees, the wind-battered headland of **St Bees Head** (RSPB; stbees.head@rspb.org.uk) is one of Cumbria's most important reserves for nesting seabirds. Depending on the season, species nesting here include fulmars, kittiwakes and razorbills, as well as Britain's only population of resident black guillemots. There are more than 2 miles of cliff paths to explore.

When you're ready to eat, you'll find snacky, filling dishes such as fried chicken, beef pot pie, and minute steak and chips at **Zest Harbourside** (01946-66981; www.zestwhitehaven.com; Low Rd; mains £12.95-19.95; 11.30am-9.30pm), a waterfront Whitehaven cafe. It also does a good line in sharing bowls and burgers. It's a popular place, from breakfast through to supper.

Egremont Crab Fair

This curious event is held in mid-September in Egremont, a little village near St Bees. The highlight of the event is the **World Gurning Championships**, in which competitors battle it out in an attempt to stretch their faces into the ugliest possible expression; the challenge is believed to stem from the 12th century, when the lord of the manor handed out sour crabapples to his workers. Famously, local Anne Wood won the trophy an impressive 24 years running till she was finally beaten in 2001.

Find out more at www.egremontcrabfair.com.

The World's Biggest Liar

Cumbrians are well known for their propensity for telling tall tales, but Will Ritson, a 19th-century landlord at the Wasdale Head Inn, took the tradition to a different level. Will was known throughout the region for his outlandish stories; one of his most famous tales concerned a Wasdale turnip that was so large that local residents burrowed into it for their Sunday lunch, and later used it as a shelter for their sheep. He also claimed to own a cross between a foxhound and a golden eagle that could leap over drystone walls.

In honour of Will's mendacious tradition, the Santon Bridge Inn holds the Biggest Liar in the World competition every November. Cumbrian dialect is allowed, but lawyers and politicians are barred from entering. One of the competition's recent winners was the TV comedian Sue Perkins, who scooped the top prize with a tale about sheep in the valley breaking wind and causing a hole in the ozone layer.

Wasdale

The road to Wasdale Head is one of the most memorable in the Lakes: you can almost feel the wildness closing in.

Hunkering beneath the brooding bulk of Scafell Pike, the **Wasdale Head Inn** (☎019467-26229; www.wasdale.com; P Wi-Fi) is a slice of hill-walking heritage: a gloriously old-fashioned 19th-century hostelry, covered in vintage photos and climbing memorabilia. The wood-panelled dining room serves fine food, with pub grub and ales from the Great Gable Brewing Co in Ritson's Bar. There are also cosy rooms (s £59, d £118–£130, tr £177), as well as roomier suites in a converted stable.

A trail leads across the field from the Wasdale Head Inn to **St Olaf's Church**. Supposedly one of the tiniest chapels in England, this 16th-century church is full of atmosphere. Legend claims the roof beams were salvaged from a Viking longboat.

Ennerdale

3 MAP 114, C2

If you really want to leave the outside world behind, the remote valley of Ennerdale is definitely the place. Just to the north of Wasdale, this valley and its namesake lake were once home to slate mines and large timber plantations, but these are slowly being removed and the valley is being returned to nature as part of the Wild Ennerdale (www.wildennerdale.co.uk) project.

Needless to say, the valley is paradise if you prefer your trails quiet. Several popular routes head over the fells to Wasdale, while walking towards Buttermere takes you past the **Black Sail YHA** (☎0845-371 9680; www.yha.org.uk; dm £35; ⊙mid-Mar–Oct, check-in 5-9pm), a marvellously remote hostel inside a shepherd's bothy. Much loved by mountaineers and hikers, it's become a YHA landmark. Space is very limited, so make sure you book ahead.

Ravenglass

4 ◉ MAP 114, B4

Ravenglass dates back to the 19th century, when the harbour was redeveloped as a link between northern England's thriving industrial ports and the iron-rich Eskdale mines to the east.

A carry over from those times and affectionately known as La'al Ratty, the pocket-sized **Ravenglass & Eskdale Railway** (☎01229-717171; www.ravenglass-railway.co.uk; adult/child/family 24hr pass £15/9/44.95; 👪) was built to ferry iron ore from the Eskdale mines to the coast. These days it's one of Cumbria's most beloved family attractions, with miniature steam trains that chug for 7 miles through the Eskdale valley between the coastal town of Ravenglass and the village of Dalegarth, and several stations in between.

East of Ravenglass, some 1.5 miles, is **Muncaster Castle** (☎01229-717614; www.muncaster.co.uk; adult/child £14.50/7.30; ⊙gardens & owl centre 10.30am-5pm, castle noon-4pm Sun-Fri), which was originally built around a 14th-century pele tower, constructed to resist raids by Reivers (p141). Home to the Pennington family for seven centuries, the castle's architectural highlights are its great hall and octagonal library, and outside you'll find an ornamental maze and splendid grounds. The crenellated castle is also home to a hawk and owl centre, which stages several flying displays a day. There's a 15% discount for booking online.

Wastwater

In his 1810 *Guide to the Lakes*, William Wordsworth described Wastwater as 'long, narrow, stern and desolate', and it's a description that still seems apt. The lake itself is owned by the National Trust and is the deepest body of water in the national park (around 79m at its deepest point). It's also the coldest, and one of the clearest; very little life can survive in its inhospitable waters, apart from the hardy Arctic char.

Muncaster Castle

Ulverston

5 MAP 114, E6

Ulverston may not have the looks of some of the Lake District's better-known towns, but in many ways Ulverston's a more authentic place, having been a merchant's town since the 13th century.

Ulverston's Stan Laurel connections (he was born here) are exhaustively explored at the quirky **Laurel & Hardy Museum** (01229-582292; www.laurel-and-hardy.co.uk; Brogden St; adult/child £5/2.50; 10am-5pm Easter-Oct, closed Mon & Wed rest of year), founded by avid Laurel and Hardy collector Bill Cubin back in 1983. This madcap museum has new premises inside the town's old Roxy cinema. It's crammed floor-to-ceiling with cinematic memorabilia, from original posters to film props, and there's a shoebox-sized cinema showing back-to-back Laurel and Hardy classics. Now run by Bill's grandson, it's a must for movie buffs.

Towering on a grassy hill above Ulverston, the **Hoad Monument** (Hoad Hill) commemorates the explorer Sir John Barrow (1764–1848), who helped map the Northwest Passage. The views of the fells and the coast are wonderful.

Two miles south of Ulverston, **Conishead Priory** (01229-584029; www.manjushri.org; free; 11am-5pm Mon-Sat, noon-5pm Sun Easter-Oct, 2-4pm Nov-Easter) has variously served as a stately home, military hospital and miners'

An Atomic Tale

Few places stir up such a maelstrom of controversy as the billowing chimneys and sprawling reactor halls of **Sellafield Nuclear Plant**, halfway between St Bees and Ravenglass. Originally an ammunitions dump and TNT factory, after WWII the nearby site of Windscale was chosen as the site for Britain's first plutonium-manufacturing reactors (needed to supply the country's nuclear arsenal). In 1956 they were joined by four Magnox reactors at Calder Hall, creating the world's first commercial nuclear power station.

Unfortunately, it also became the site of the world's first nuclear accident: in 1957 a fire tore through the Windscale reactor hall forcing its emergency closure. Radioactive material eventually drifted as far afield as Wales, Scotland and the Irish west coast.

It was the first of a long line of controversies. The Windscale site, subsequently renamed Sellafield in 1981 and now the UK's largest nuclear-reprocessing facility, has been dogged by nonstop claims of environmental damage and radioactive pollution over the last 50 years – not least by the Irish government, who have long campaigned for an embargo on the release of reactor water into the Irish Sea.

With a new generation of British nuclear power stations on the horizon, Sellafield's own future is still very much in the balance. The site has been undergoing a gradual decommissioning process over recent years, but as yet, no final decision has been taken on whether a replacement will be built.

hostel, but it now houses a Kadampa Buddhist temple and Europe's largest bronze Buddha. Guided tours (£3.60) run on weekends at 2.30pm.

Further afield, some 8½ miles southwest of Ulverston, the rosy ruins of **Furness Abbey** (EH; ☎01229-823420; www.english-heritage.org.uk/visit/places/furness-abbey; adult/child £5.70/3.40; ⏰10am-6pm) are all that remain of one of northern England's largest and most powerful monasteries. Founded in the 12th century, it met an ignominious end in 1537 during the dissolution of the monasteries. You can make out its footprint: arches, windows and some transept walls are still standing, along with the shell of the bell tower.

In business since 1892, the lovely old-fashioned **Gillams Tearoom** (☎01229-587564; www.gillams-tearoom.co.uk; 64 Market St; lunches £4-12; ⏰9am-5pm Mon-Sat) serves delicious veggie-organic food, which is very much of the moment – hot quiches, savoury tarts, fresh soups, quinoa salads. Luxury biscuits, jams and other foodie souvenirs are sold in the grocer's shop next door.

For a quick all-day breakfast, a proper cottage pie or a lovely omelette, Ulverston locals rate **Poppies Cafe** (☎01229-583134; www.poppiescafe.co.uk; 4 Union St; mains £6.95-7.95; ⌚9am-3pm Wed-Sat), a decent lunch stop in Ulverston. It also does an 'afternoon cheese' session (£14.99), featuring local cheeses, a pork pie and a glass of wine.

Basic pub grub is on offer at centrally located **Farmers Arms** (☎01229-584469; www.thefarmers-ulverston.co.uk; 3 Market Pl; mains £9.95-15.95), on Ulverston's main market square.

Cartmel

6 MAP 114, F6

Medieval **Cartmel Priory** (free; ⌚9am-5.30pm May-Oct, to 3.30pm Nov-Apr) is one of only a handful to have survived the ravages of the dissolution of the monasteries largely unscathed. Its most unusual feature is its square belfry tower, set diagonally across from the original lantern tower. Inside, light filters through the stained-glass east window, lighting up the wooden pews and stone tombs set into the floor. Note the skulls and hourglasses carved into many tombstones, designed to remind parishioners of the transience of life.

Cartmel Priory

Without a doubt Cumbria's best-known restaurant, **L'Enclume** (015395-36362; www.lenclume.co.uk; Cavendish St; set lunch £59, lunch & dinner menu £155; noon-1.30pm & 6.30-8.30pm Tue-Sun) is run by the wildly imaginative chef Simon Rogan (often dubbed Cumbria's answer to Heston Blumenthal). Known for his boundary-pushing cuisine and off-the-wall presentation, Rogan's dishes often have a focus on foraged ingredients such as sea buckthorn, juniper, dandelion seed and Douglas fir. Reservations should be made months in advance.

An alternative (and affordable) way to experience Rogan's culinary flair is at his village bistro **Rogan & Company** (015395-35917; www.roganandcompany.co.uk; The Square; 2-/3-course set lunch £20/26, mains £18-25; noon-2pm & 6-9pm Mon & Wed-Sat, 12.15-3.15pm Sun). Here the menu focuses on classic British dishes such as pork belly, butter-poached cod and roasted plaice, perfected and perfectly presented. It's cosy and welcoming, with fires and wooden interiors, and the Sunday roast is an utter feast.

Upmarket **Cartmel Village Shop** (015395-36280; www.

Morecambe Bay Crossing

Before the coming of the railway, the sandy expanse of Morecambe Bay provided the only reliable route into the Lake District from the south of England.

The traditional crossing is made from Arnside on the eastern side of the bay over to Kents Bank, near Grange-over-Sands. It has, however, always been a risky journey. Over 115 sq miles of tidal sand and mud flats (the largest such area in Britain) are revealed at low tide, but the bay is notorious for its treacherous quicksands and fast-rising tide (said to move at the speed of a galloping horse).

Even experienced fishermen have lost carts, ponies and tractors in the capricious sands, and there have been numerous strandings, including a notorious incident in 2004, when at least 21 Chinese cockle pickers were tragically caught by the tide and drowned.

It's possible to walk across the flats at low tide, but only in the company of the official Queen's Guide, a role established in 1536. Cedric Robinson, a local fisherman, is the 25th official Queen's Guide, and leads walks across the sands throughout the year. You'll need to register a fortnight in advance; ask at the Grange tourist office for details of the next crossing. The 8-mile trudge takes around 3½ hours.

Find out more at www.morecambebay.org.uk.

L'Enclume

cartmelvillageshop.co.uk; 1 The Square; 9am-5pm Mon-Sat, 10am-4.30pm Sun) developed the recipe for sticky toffee pudding – accept no substitute. You can buy it to cook at home and it also comes in ginger, banana and chocolate versions. Lots of other Cumbrian goodies such as cheeses and chutneys are also sold here.

Fromage fans will be in seventh heaven at **Cartmel Cheeses** (015395-34307; www.cartmelcheeses.co.uk; 1 Unsworth Yard Brewery; 9.30am-5pm Mon-Sat, 10am-4.30pm Sun), a fine cheese emporium with a particular focus on producers from northern England.

Driving Tour

Wrynose & Hardknott Passes

Is this the nation's most spectacular drive? Many seasoned drivers seem to think so, and you certainly won't be the only one doing it on a summer weekend. Traversing both of the steepest passes in England and reaching 30% gradients in some places, it's a real roller coaster.

Drive Facts

Start Ambleside

End Boot

Length 39 miles; three hours

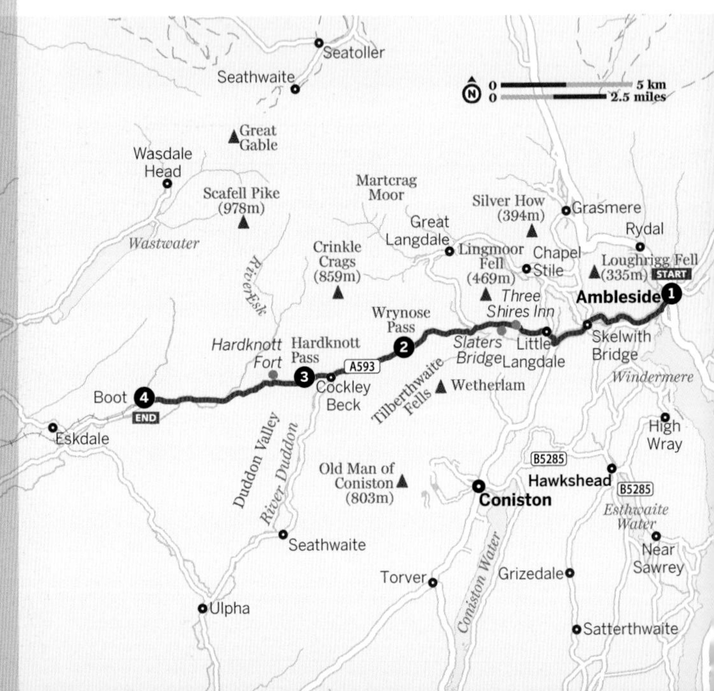

❶ Ambleside to Little Langdale

You can do the drive in either direction, but east–west gives you the best views. Be prepared for other drivers coming the opposite way.

Start out in **Ambleside** and follow the A593 to **Skelwith Bridge**, stopping for breakfast at Chesters by the River (p60) and a stroll to Skelwith Force. Just after Skelwith Bridge, take the sharp right-hand turn onto the steep road into **Little Langdale**.

❷ Wrynose Pass

It's here where things get steep. The road crawls up towards Little Langdale Tarn, offering increasingly wild views of Wetherlam and the Tilberthwaite Fells as it passes the **Three Shires Inn**. You can pause here and take a walk to the quaint packhorse crossing at **Slaters Bridge**, then continue the climb up to **Wrynose Pass**. At the top of the pass, the views across the fells become increasingly wild and empty, and you'll really start to feel like you've left civilisation a long way behind. Near the summit is a small car park containing the **Three Shire Stone**, where the counties of Cumberland, Westmorland and Lancashire historically met.

❸ Hardknott Pass

From Wrynose, the road plunges into Cockley Beck. You'll pass a left-hand fork leading towards Duddon Valley; ignore this and follow the right-hand fork, tracing a series of long hairpins up to **Hardknott Pass** at 393m. The vistas here are magnificent: you'll be able to see all the way to the coast on a clear day.

❹ Boot

From the pass, the road drops into another set of very sharp, steep hairpins, passing the Roman ruins of **Hardknott Fort**, before dropping down into the green sweep of **Eskdale**. Have a pint at one of the pubs around **Boot** – you've earned it.

Explore

Inland Cumbria

Many visitors speed through the northern and eastern reaches of Cumbria in a headlong dash for the Lake District, but it's worth taking the time to venture inland from the national park. It might not have the big-name fells and chocolate-box villages, but it's full of interest, with traditional towns, crumbling castles, abandoned abbeys and sweeping moors set alongside the magnificent Roman engineering project of Hadrian's Wall.

Carlisle makes the most obvious base. Make early morning visits to Carlisle Castle (p132), Carlisle Cathedral (p129) and Tullie House Museum (p129), followed by brunch at Foxes Cafe Lounge (p133). Then hop in the car (or catch a train) to spend the afternoon in Kendal, where you should visit Kendal Museum (p140) and the Abbot Hall Art Gallery (p140). If you have a car, don't miss the superb food hall at Low Sizergh Barn (p143). Have dinner at the Moon Highgate (p142), then catch a late film at the Brewery Arts Centre (p143).

Getting There & Around

Carlisle, Kendal and Penrith are easy to reach by car thanks to their proximity to the M6 motorway. There are large car parks near all the town centres.

All three towns are on the west-coast line from London to Glasgow. Carlisle is also the terminus for the Cumbrian Coast and Tyne Valley lines, and the Settle to Carlisle Railway (p131).

Inland Cumbria Map on p136

Carlisle Cathedral (p129) JACEK WOJNAROWSKI / SHUTTERSTOCK ©

Top Sights

Carlisle

Carlisle has history and heritage aplenty. Precariously perched on the frontier between England and Scotland, in the area once ominously dubbed the 'Debatable Lands', Cumbria's capital is a city with a notoriously stormy past: sacked by the Vikings, pillaged by the Scots and plundered by the Border Reivers, the city has been on the front line of England's defences for more than 1000 years.

City Sights

Aside from Carlisle Castle (p132), there are a couple of other sights worth a look. Carlisle's flagship museum, the **Tullie House Museum** (01228-618718; www.tulliehouse.co.uk; Castle St; adult/child £6.50/free; 10am-5pm Mon-Sat, 11am-5pm Sun), covers 2000 years of the city's past. The Roman Frontier Gallery explores Carlisle's Roman foundations, while the Border Galleries cover the Bronze Age through to the Industrial Revolution. Two galleries flesh out the story: the Border Reivers covers the marauding bandits who once terrorised the area, while the Vikings Revealed exhibition displays finds from the Cumwhitton Viking cemetery, including helmets, swords and grave goods. The top-floor Lookout has cracking views of the castle.

Built from the same red sandstone as Carlisle Castle, **Carlisle Cathedral** (pictured; 01228-548151; www.carlislecathedral.org.uk; 7 The Abbey; suggested donation £5, photography £1; 7.30am-6.15pm Mon-Sat, to 5pm Sun) began life as a priory church in 1122 and became a cathedral when its first abbot, Athelwold, became the first bishop of Carlisle. Among its notable features are the 15th-century choir stalls, the barrel-vaulted roof and the 14th-century East Window, one of the largest Gothic windows in England. Surrounding the cathedral are other priory relics, including the 16th-century **fratry** and the **prior's tower**.

Fine Food Options

Carlisle has plenty of choice when it comes to pubs and curry houses, but it pays to be a bit more selective when it comes to its fine-dining restaurants.

The **Thin White Duke** (01228-402334; www.thinwhiteduke.info; 1 Devonshire St; mains £9.95-14.95; 11.45am-11pm) scores points for the name alone (at least for Bowie fans), although the Duke himself would have been most

★ Top Tips

Tours of Carlisle and the surrounding area (including Hadrian's Wall) with **Open Book Visitor Guiding** (01228-670578; www.greatguidedtours.co.uk) can be arranged through the **Carlisle Tourist Office** (01228-598596; www.discovercarlisle.co.uk; 9.30am-5pm Mon-Sat, 10.30am-4pm Sun).

unlikely to tuck into the burgers, tandoori chicken and flat-iron steak on the menu. He might have liked the cocktails, though, and the location – in a former monastery, with plenty of exposed brick and ramshackle-chic decor.

Low and slow; pig, chicken and cow. That pretty much sums up the **Foxborough Smokehouse** (☎01228-317925; www.foxboroughrestaurant.com; 52 Cecil St; mains lunch £10, dinner £12-16; ⏰noon-2pm & 5-9pm Wed & Thu, noon-2pm & 5-10pm Fri, 10am-10pm Sat, noon-2pm & 5-8.30pm Sun), where everything is spiced, full-on-flavoured and unashamedly meaty. The house special is the Jacob's Ladder – dry-aged beef short rib cooked for aeons in a 'green egg' cooker. Vegetarians have options – salads, chilli – but this is one for meat eaters, really.

For many years **David's** (☎01228-523578; www.davidsrestaurant.co.uk; 62 Warwick Rd; 2-course lunch £17.95, dinner mains £16.95-25.95; ⏰noon-3.30pm & 6.30-11pm Tue-Sat) has been the address for formal dining in Carlisle and there's no sign that's going to change. It majors in rich, traditional dishes with a strong French flavour: lamb with a pistachio crust and port gravy, roast chicken with leek and tarragon mash. The house is full of period architecture, too.

Another popular option is the quirkily named gastropub the **Last Zebra** (☎01228-593600; www.thelastzebra.co.uk; 6 Lowther St; mains £10-12; ⏰11am-midnight Mon-Sat, noon-midnight Sun), good for early evening drinks and a plate of grub such as *steak-frites* (steak and fries), buttermilk chicken burger or '80s-style chicken Kiev. Fancy it isn't, but it's a

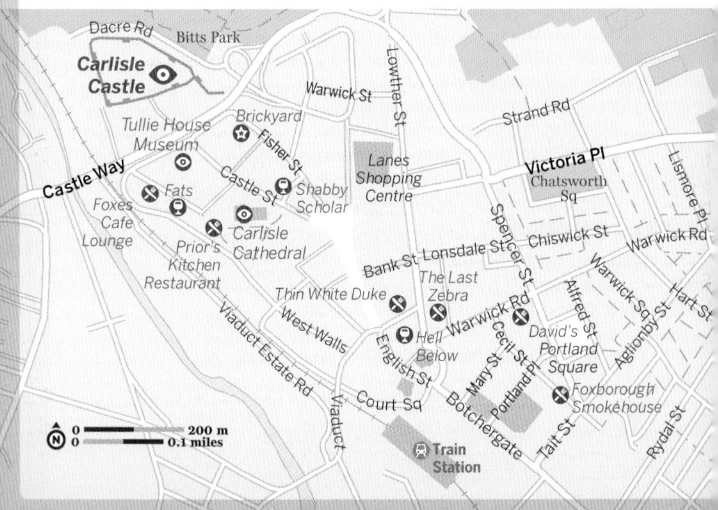

Settle to Carlisle Railway

Britain has its fair share of classic railway journeys, but few can match the history and heritage of the **Settle-Carlisle Railway** (www.settle-carlisle.co.uk; adult return £28), which rattles across the Yorkshire Dales and the Eden Valley from Leeds to Carlisle, with stops at Settle, Kirkby Stephen and Appleby.

It's one of England's most stunning train journeys, traversing a varied landscape of moor, heath, pasture and valley, not to mention 14 tunnels and the 24-arched Ribblehead viaduct, one of the great triumphs of Victorian engineering.

The line required the blood, sweat and graft of 6000 'navvies' to complete at a cost of £3.5 million (twice the original estimate), and work was halted several times due to freezing weather conditions, floods, blizzards and even a smallpox outbreak. The railway was finally opened for business in 1876. Over a century later in 1998, a memorial stone was laid in the churchyard of St Mary's in Mallerstang to commemorate the scores of workers who lost their lives during its construction.

lively, buzzy spot and the building (once a bank) is interesting – check out the great skylight.

When in need of a beverage, the brick-walled bar **Hell Below** (☎01228-548481; 14-16 Devonshire St; ⏰noon-midnight Mon-Fri, to 2am Sat, to 6pm Sun) is a popular haunt for Carlisle's hipster drinkers, with craft beers and a bargain cocktail menu (with fun concoctions to try such as bubblegum sours and starburst cosmos). Snacky food – burgers, nachos, pizzas and the like – will fill a hole if you're hungry.

Also popular is the **Shabby Scholar** (☎01228-402813; 11-13 Carlyle Court; tapas £3-7, lunch mains £7-9.50; ⏰10am-midnight Mon-Sat), decked out with scruffy furniture, a bar made out of old crates and a determinedly chilled vibe. It's fine for tapas, light bites and burgers, but many people just come for cocktails.

A less hectic alternative to Botchergate's pubs, **Fats** (☎01228-511774; 48 Abbey St; ⏰11am-11pm) regularly hosts DJs and comedy nights.

And if it's music you're after, try **Brickyard** (☎01228-512220; www.thebrickyardonline.com; 14 Fisher St), Carlisle's grungy gig venue housed in the former Memorial Hall.

Top Sights

Carlisle Castle

Carlisle was founded as a military city, and its brooding, rust-red castle provides a timely reminder of the conflicts that have shaped the city's history. For 500 years until the Act of Union in 1603, it was the frontline fortress in several Anglo-Scottish conflicts.

MAP P134

01228-591922

www.english-heritage.org.uk/visit/places/carlisle-castle

Castle Way

adult/child £8/4.80

10am-6pm Apr-Sep, to 5pm Oct-Mar

History

Founded around a Celtic and Roman stronghold, the castle's Norman keep was added in 1092 by William II (aka 'William Rufus'), and later refortified by subsequent monarchs including Henry II, Edward I and Henry VIII (who added the supposedly cannon-proof circular towers).

The castle has witnessed many dramatic events over the centuries – famously, it has endured more sieges than any other castle in Britain. In 1315 the English-held castle was encircled by Robert the Bruce after his victory at Bannockburn, but the castle sat out the siege under its commander, Andrew Harclay. Another bloody siege occurred in 1461, during the Wars of the Roses, when an army of Lancastrians and Scots pounded the Yorkist defenders with artillery.

Mary, Queen of Scots, was briefly imprisoned here in 1568. Another notorious eight-month siege occurred during the Civil War in 1644, when the 700-strong Royalist garrison were starved into submission by the parliamentarian General Lesley; the defenders survived by eating rats, mice and the castle dogs before finally surrendering in 1645 (a day-by-day account was kept by 18-year-old Isaac Tullie, after whom the city's Tullie House Museum is named). The Jacobite siege of 1745 was less protracted: Bonnie Prince Charlie's army besieged Carlisle for just six days before the defenders caved in.

During the 19th century, the castle became a military barracks, and the headquarters of the Border Regiment, one of the oldest in the British Army.

The Outer Defences

Like most British castles, the layout of the castle has changed several times during its 900-year history. Notable features to look out for include the **Outer Gatehouse** (sometimes

★ Top Tips

- A combined ticket covering Carlisle Castle and Cumbria's Museum of Military Life costs £9.20/5.15.

Take a Break

There are several cafes within easy reach of the castle. The trendy **Foxes Cafe Lounge** (01228-491836; www.foxescafelounge.co.uk; 18 Abbey St; mains £4-8; 9am-4pm Mon-Fri, 10am-4.30pm Sat) is great for a pastry and cappuccino or an Apple Refresher smoothie – or better still, settle in for a hearty brunch (available in Full Fox carnivorous and Herbivore veggie versions).

Or try the old-fashioned **Prior's Kitchen Restaurant** (Carlisle Cathedral; lunches £4-6; 9.45am-4pm Mon-Sat) for quiches, salads and afternoon teas, all served in the cathedral's fratry, once used as a monk's mess hall.

called De Ireby's Tower) and the **Captain's Tower**, which both date from around the 14th century; the impressive **Half-Moon Battery**, added by Moravian engineer Stefan von Haschenperg in 1542; and the **Inner Ward**, which served as a second line of defence in case the castle's outer defences were breached.

The Keep

The stout sandstone **keep**, sometimes called the Great Tower, is the central point of Carlisle Castle. Its square-sided design is typical of Anglo-Norman castles, but it has been altered and adapted many times. It is now four storeys high, and contains a series of displays outlining the castle's history. From the roof, there are stupendous views over Carlisle and the Scottish borders beyond.

Look out for some **medieval carvings** (pictured) on the second floor and the 'licking stones' in the **dungeon**, which Jacobite prisoners supposedly lapped for moisture during their incarceration in 1746.

Cumbria's Museum of Military Life

Contained inside the walls of the castle, this **museum** (☎01228-532774; adult/child £4.50/2.50, combined ticket with Carlisle Castle £9.20/5.15; ⏰10am-6pm Apr-Oct, to 5pm Sat-Thu Nov-Mar) explores the county's proud military history, with weapons, medals, standards, uniforms and other artefacts associated with the region's regiment – from its beginnings as the 34th Regiment of Foot in 1702 through to its current incarnation as the Duke of Lancaster's regiment. The flagship exhibit is a reconstruction of a WWI trench, a full-blown audiovisual experience.

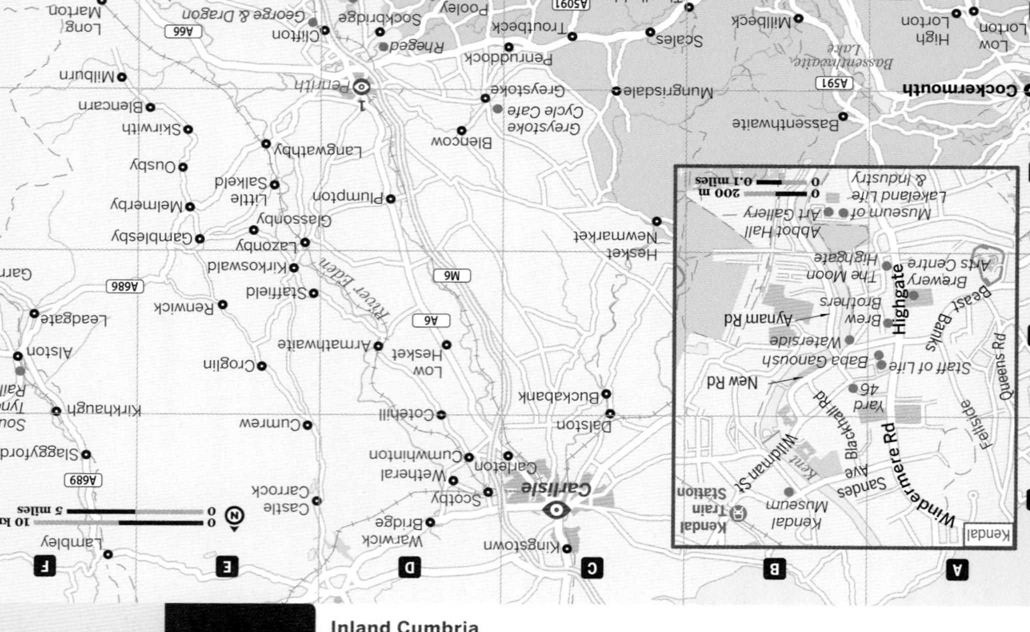
A
B
C
D
E
F
1
2
3
4
10 km
5 miles
Lambley
A689
Slaggyford
South
Tynedale
Railway
Kirkhaugh
Alston
Leadgate
Garrigill
A686
Castle
Carrock
Cumrew
Croglin
Renwick
Staffield
Kirkoswald
Lazonby
Glassonby
Gamblesby
Melmerby
Little
Salkeld
Ousby
Skirwith
Blencarn
Milburn
Langwathby
Long
Marton
Brampton
A66
River Eden
Warwick
Bridge
Scotby
Wetheral
Cumwhinton
Cotehill
Armathwaite
Low
Hesket
A6
M6
Plumpton
Penrith
Clifton
George & Dragon
Lowther
Allium at
Askham Hall
Kingstown
Carlisle
Carleton
Dalston
Buckabank
Hesket
Newmarket
Blencow
Greystoke
Cycle Cafe
Greystoke
Penruddock
Rheged
Sockbridge
Askham
Lowther
Estate
Pooley
Bridge
Troutbeck
A5091
Watermillock
Dockray
Mungrisdale
Scales
Threlkeld
Bassenthwaite
A591
Millbeck
Keswick
Derwentwater
Bassenthwaite
Lake
Cockermouth
High
Lorton
Low
Lorton
B5292
Braithwaite
Thackthwaite
Swinside
Loweswater
Kendal
Kendal
Train
Station
Kendal
Museum
Wildman St
Kent
Sandes
Ave
Blackhall Rd
New Rd
Windermere Rd
Yard
46
Baba Ganoush
Waterside
Aynam Rd
Staff of Life
Brew
Brothers
Highgate
The Moon
Highgate
Abbot Hall
Art Gallery
Museum of
Lakeland Life
& Industry
Brewery
Arts Centre
Beast
Banks
Fellside
Queens Rd
200 m
0.1 miles

A
B
C
D
E
F
5
6
7
8
Croasdale
Crummock Water
Newlands Valley
Buttermere
Gatesgarth
Ennerdale Water
Borrowdale
Seatoller
Seathwaite
Lodore
Grange
Watendlath
Rosthwaite
Stonethwaite
Thirlmere
Thirlspot
Glenridding
Patterdale
Ullswater
Howtown
Martindale
Bampton
Shap
Appleby-in-Westmorland
A592
A591
A6
M6
Hawsewater
Lake District National Park
Wasdale Head
Scafell Pike (987m)
River Esk
Wastwater
Nether Wasdale
Cumbrian Mountains
Grasmere
Elterwater
Ambleside
Skelwith Bridge
Troutbeck
Troutbeck Bridge
Kentmere
Kentmere Reservoir
River Kent
Tebay
Forest Hall
Ravenstonedale
Newbiggin-on-Line
Yorkshire Dales National Park
Boot
Eskdale
Cockley Beck
Seathwaite
Broad Oak
Ulpha
Torver
Coniston
Hawkshead
Near Sawrey
Grizedale
Coniston Water
Windermere
Bowness-on-Windermere
Ings
Staveley
Ferry Nab
Winster
Crosthwaite
Wheatsheaf Inn
Kendal
Low Sizergh Barn
Sizergh Castle
Killington Lake
Sedbergh
Millthrop
Gawthrop
Dent
Barbon
Milnthorpe
Heaves
Around Kendal
Levens Hall
Witherslack
High Newton
A590
Bowland Bridge
Lakeside
Newby Bridge
Rusland
Bouth
Haverthwaite
Gawthwaite
Grizebeck
Foxfield
Broughton-in-Furness
A5084
A593
River Duddon
Bootle
Silecroft
A595

Penrith

1 MAP P136 D4

Just outside the borders of the national park, Penrith perhaps has more in common with the stout market towns of the Yorkshire Dales. It's a solid, traditional place with plenty of cosy pubs and quaint teashops and a lively market on Tuesdays. It's also the main gateway for exploring the picturesque Eden Valley.

The ruins of **Penrith Castle** (7.30am-9pm Easter-Oct, to 4.30pm Nov-Easter) loom on the edge of town opposite the train station. Built in the 14th century by William Strickland (later Bishop of Carlisle and Archbishop of Canterbury), it was expanded by Richard III to resist Scottish raids, one of which razed the town in 1345.

Cunningly disguised as a Lakeland hill 2 miles west of Penrith, the visitor centre of **Rheged** (01768-868000; www.rheged.com; 10am-6pm) houses an IMAX cinema and temporary exhibitions. There's also a large retail hall selling Cumbrian foodstuffs and souvenirs.

The sprawling **Lowther Estate** (01931-712192; www.lowthercastle.

Hadrian's Wall

Named in honour of the emperor who ordered it built, Hadrian's Wall was one of Rome's greatest engineering projects. This enormous 73-mile-long wall was built between AD 122 and 128 to protect the Roman-controlled south from the warlike Scottish Picts. When completed, it ran from the Solway Firth on the Cumbrian Coast almost to the mouth of the Tyne in the east.

Every Roman mile (0.95 miles) there was a gateway guarded by a small fort (milecastle). Several of these still survive, including the once-formidable **Birdoswald Roman Fort** (EH; 01697-747602; www.english-heritage.org.uk; adult/child £8.30/5; 10am-6pm Apr-Sep, to 5pm Oct, to 4pm Sat & Sun Nov–mid-Feb, to 4pm Wed-Sun mid-Feb–Mar), on an escarpment overlooking the Irthing Gorge along a minor road off the B6318, 4 miles west of Greenhead in Cumbria.

Known as Banna to the Romans, it marks the start of the longest intact stretch of wall, extending from here to Harrows Scar Milecastle. Built to replace an earlier timber-and-turf fort, Birdoswald would have been the operating base for around 1000 Roman soldiers; excavations have revealed three of the four gateways, as well as granary stores, workshops, exterior walls and a military drill hall. The surviving 4m-high gatehouse leads to various interactive, kid-friendly exhibits. There's also a cafe and shop.

CRAIG STENNETT / ALAMY STOCK PHOTO ©

Staff of Life bakery (p141)

org; adult/child £9/7; 10am-5pm) once belonged to one of the Lake District's most venerable families and is currently undergoing a huge, multi-million-pound restoration project. The 400-year-old crenellated castle and the estate's grounds are now open to the public again. Though the castle itself is to remain a ruin, restoration work is gradually breathing life back into the gardens, which have been largely forgotten since the estate fell into disrepair following WWII. It hosts the **Kendal Calling** (www.kendalcalling.co.uk; Jul) music festival. Lowther Estate is also home to **George & Dragon** (01768-865381; www.georgeanddragonclifton.co.uk; Clifton; mains £13.95-21.95; noon-2.30pm & 6-9pm), a pretty pub that sources much of its produce (including game) from there. Fires, benches and rafters make for a cosy setting and the food is generally good, if not quite gastropub standard.

If you're going to eat out in Penrith town, **Four & Twenty** (01768-210231; www.fourandtwentypenrith.co.uk; 14 King St; lunch mains £14-16, dinner mains £16.50-19.50; noon-2.30pm & 6-9.30pm Tue-Sat) is the place to do it. Proper fine dining with a reasonable price tag is the modus operandi at this bistro, which blends sleek decor with rustic wood, banquette seats and mix-and-match furniture. Expect sophisticated dishes such as pork tenderloin with garlic, sage and Parma ham, or sea bass 'bouillabaisse-style'.

There's been a grocer here since 1793 and the endear-

South Tynedale Railway

The heritage narrow-gauge **South Tynedale Railway** (01434-381696, timetable 01434-382828; www.south-tynedale-railway.org.uk; adult/child/family rover ticket £10/5/25; Apr-Oct) – the highest such railway in England – puffs for 3.5 miles of scenic track between Alston and Lintley in Northumberland. En route you pass over three landmark viaducts at South Tyne, Gilderdale and Whitley.

ingly old-fashioned **JJ Graham** (01768-862281; www.jjgraham.co.uk; 6-7 Market Sq; 8.30am-5.30pm Mon-Sat) deli is still the place to pick up treats such as local cheeses, homemade chutneys and loose-leaf teas.

Outside of Penrith, in the village of Askham, is **Allium at Askham Hall** 01931-712350; www.askhamhall.co.uk; Askham; dinner menu £50; 7-9.30pm Tue-Sat), boasting a regal setting and royally good dining showcasing Chef Richard Swale's passion for Cumbrian produce, which was learned from a childhood spent shooting, fishing and foraging. His food combines richness and delicacy – such as chicken, cauliflower cheese and truffles – and everything looks like a work of art. The setting inside the hall is quite formal; dress nicely.

Kendal

2 MAP P136 D7

Technically Kendal isn't in the Lake District, but it's a major gateway town. Often known as the 'Auld Grey Town' thanks to the sombre grey stone used for many of its buildings, Kendal is a bustling shopping centre with some good restaurants, a funky arts centre and intriguing museums.

Founded in 1796 by the inveterate Victorian collector William Todhunter, the mixed-bag **Kendal Museum** (01539-815597; www.kendalmuseum.org.uk; Station Rd; £2; 10am-4pm Tue-Sat) features everything from stuffed beasts and transfixed butterflies to medieval coin hoards. There's also a reconstruction of the office of Alfred Wainwright, who served as honorary curator at the museum from 1945 to 1974: look out for his knapsack and well-chewed pipe.

Kendal's **Abbot Hall Art Gallery** (01539-722464; www.abbothall.org.uk; adult/child £7/free, joint ticket with Museum of Lakeland Life & Industry £9; 10.30am-5pm Mon-Sat Apr-Oct, to 4pm Nov-Mar) houses one of the northwest's best collections of 18th- and 19th-century fine art. It's especially strong on portraiture and Lakeland landscapes: look out for works by Constable, John Ruskin and local boy George Romney, who was born in Dalton-in-Furness in 1734 and became a sought-after portraitist, as well as a key figure in the 'Kendal School'.

Directly opposite Abbot Hall, the **Museum of Lakeland Life & Industry** (☎01539-722464; www.lakelandmuseum.org.uk; adult/child £5/free, joint ticket with Abbot Hall Art Gallery £9; ⏰10.30am-5pm Mon-Sat Mar-Oct, to 4pm Nov-Feb) re-creates various scenes from Lakeland life during the 18th and 19th centuries, including a farmhouse parlour, a Lakeland kitchen, an apothecary and the study of Arthur Ransome, author of *Swallows and Amazons* – look out for some of his original sketchbooks.

When you're ready to refuel, options abound.

Staff of Life (☎01539-738606; www.staffoflifebakery.co.uk; 2 Berry's Yard; bread from £2; ⏰8.30am-4pm Mon-Sat) is the place to come for fresh bread and pastries – elderflower sourdoughs, deli ryes, *pane rustica* and classic whole-meal loaves. It also runs bread-making courses at least once a month (£100 for a day's course).

The hipster cafe comes to Kendal at this new number on Highgate, **Brew Brothers** (☎01539-722237; www.brew-brothers.co.uk; 69 Highgate; mains £8.50-10; ⏰8.30am-5.30pm Mon-Sat). With its scruffy wood furniture and black-aproned baristas, it's got the aesthetic down, but its owners are Lakeland through and

The Border Reivers

During the early Middle Ages, the Anglo-Scottish border was a pretty anarchic place. Sporadic conflicts and cross-border raids were common, and rival families of 'Border Reivers' indulged in a bloodthirsty campaign of violence, looting and pillaging, earning the area around Carlisle the ominous nickname of the 'Debatable Lands'.

The Reivers usually attacked within a day's ride north or south of the border. They chose their targets carefully, favouring places without royal or aristocratic protection, especially those which were unlikely to put up a fight (abbeys and priories were particularly popular).

Winter was the key season for raiding, when the long nights gave the Reivers the maximum time to do their dirty work. They plundered anything and everything, from crops, cereals and horses to money, jewellery and expensive ornaments. Some goods were kept, while others were sold or bartered for weapons, armour and raiding equipment.

Reiving died out from around the middle of the 18th century, but Reiver family names are still widespread across the Scottish borders, Northumberland and Cumbria: you can see a list of the most common at www.landsbeyondthewall.co.uk/names.html.

The Reivers also contributed a number of words to the English language, including 'blackmail' and, of course, 'bereaved'.

through – they previously ran a cafe in Windermere. Go for smashed avocado and poached eggs for brekkie, then for lunch try a hot smoked-salmon sandwich. Yum.

Down a side alley, **Baba Ganoush** (☎01539-738210; www.baba-ganoush.co.uk; Finkle St; mains £5-9; ⊙10.30am-3pm Tue-Sat) is a Mediterranean-inspired cafe serving up delicious lunches of felafels, lamb stews, veggie meze and Moroccan tagines, plus a big range of salads. It's recently moved a little way down the street to give more space for diners.

Now run by prodigiously talented chef Leon Whitehead, the **Moon Highgate** (☎01539-729254; www.themoonhighgate.com; 129 Highgate; lunch £6-12, dinner £17-21; ⊙11.30am-2.15pm Tue-Sat & 5.30-9.15pm Tue-Fri, 6-9.30pm Sat) is a smart bistro which takes its cue from the seasons and the pick of Cumbrian produce. Classic flavours sit alongside surprises: watercress panna cotta, or hen's egg with onion broth. Dishes are beautifully plated, veggie choice is good and the uncluttered space is a winner. The town's top table.

Kendal is well stocked with cafes, but **Yard 46** (☎07585-320522; www.yard46.co.uk; Branthwaite Brow; lunches £3-8; ⊙10am-4pm Mon-Fri, to 5pm Sat) is a gem well worth seeking out. It's down a blink-and-you'll-miss-it alleyway, with a little courtyard and an old whitewashed building with cruck-framed attic dining room. Delicious soups, imaginative salads and yummy cakes, plus unusual options such as *pan con tomate* (tomato bruschetta) and veggie brunch baps with a fried duck's egg.

Kendal's veggies make a beeline for **Waterside** (☎01539-729743;

Sizergh Castle

Low Sizergh Barn

A prodigious selection of Lakeland goodies are available at this fantastic **farm shop** (www.lowsizerghbarn.co.uk; 9am-5.30pm), just outside Kendal on the A590. There's also a farm trail and woodland walk, and you can watch the cows being milked – look out for the raw-milk vending machine beside the shop entrance. Only in Cumbria!

www.watersidekendal.co.uk; Kent View; light meals £4-10; 8.30am-4.30pm Mon-Sat), a riverside cafe, and an old fave for filling sandwiches, flapjacks and naughty-but-nice cakes.

The cracking **Brewery Arts Centre** (01539-725133; www.breweryarts.co.uk; Highgate) – with a gallery, cafe, theatre and two cinemas, hosting the latest films as well as music, theatre, dance and much more – has no shortage of options for an evening out. Its restaurant, **Grain Store** (01539-725133; Highgate; pizzas £6.50-10, mains £8-16.50; 10am-11pm Mon-Sat), does a decent line in pub grub and stone-baked pizzas, perfect for a quick prefilm or pretheatre supper.

Around Kendal

3 MAP P136 D8

South of Kendal you'll find a couple of sights worth checking out.

The Elizabethan manor of **Levens Hall** (015395-60321; www.levenshall.co.uk; house & gardens adult/child £13.90/5, gardens only £9.90/4; house noon-4pm, gardens 10am-5pm Sun-Thu Mar-Oct) was built around a mid-13th-century fortified pele tower, and fine Jacobean furniture litters its interior, although the real draw is the 17th-century topiary garden – a surreal riot of pyramids, swirls, curls, pompoms and peacocks straight out of *Alice in Wonderland*.

Three-and-a-half miles south of Kendal along the A591, **Sizergh Castle** (NT; 015395-60070; www.nationaltrust.org.uk/sizergh; adult/child £11.50/5.75, gardens only £7.50/3.75; house noon-4pm Apr-Oct, gardens 10am-5pm) is the feudal seat of the Strickland family. Set around a pele tower, its finest asset is the lavish wood panelling on display in the Inlaid Chamber, as well as a huge 650-hectare estate encompassing lakes, orchards, woods and pastureland.

A sister pub to the marvellous Mason's Arms (p45) near Windermere, the **Wheatsheaf Inn** (015395-68938; www.thewheatsheafbrigsteer.co.uk; Brigsteer; mains £10.50-16.50; 11am-11pm) is a classic pub near the Lyth Valley has a great reputation for its grub. Dishes are pubby rather than gourmet, but tasty – go for a meaty or fishy 'oak plank' to share, or a hearty fish pie or 12-hour braised brisket. It's 5 miles southwest of Kendal.

Survival Guide

Scafell Pike (p112) from the summit of Pillar STEWART SMITH / ALAMY STOCK PHOTO ©

Before You Go

Book Your Stay

Booking your accommodation in advance is recommended, especially in summer, at weekends and on islands (where options are often limited). Book at least two months ahead for July and August.

B&Bs These small, family-run houses generally provide good value. More luxurious versions are more like a boutique hotel.

Hotels Hotels range from half a dozen rooms above a pub to restored country houses and castles, with a commensurate range of rates.

Hostels There's a good choice of both institutional and independent hostels, many housed in rustic and/or historic buildings.

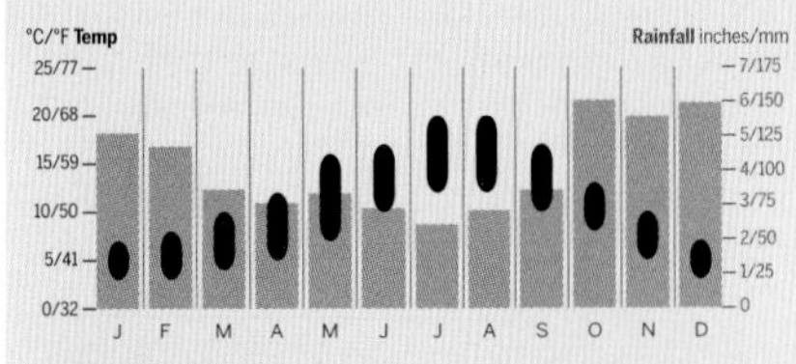

When to Go

- The Lake District is the UK's most popular national park; visit in early spring and late autumn for the smallest crowds.
- The weather is notoriously fickle – showers can strike at any time of year, so bring wet-weather gear just in case.
- Cumbria's largest mountain festival is held in Keswick in mid-May, while the Beer Festival in June welcomes ale aficionados from across the globe.
- In November the world's greatest liars congregate on Santon Bridge for their annual fibbing contest.

Useful Websites

Go Lakes (www.golakes.co.uk) The regional tourist board is a useful place to start your search, and will arrange bookings for a small fee.

Cumbrian Cottages (www.cumbrian-cottages.co.uk) Offers more than 900 rental properties, including deluxe, pet-friendly and family-specific choices.

National Trust Campsite Bookings (www.nationaltrust.org.uk/features/lake-district-camping) Online bookings for the Trust's four excellent campsites.

Best Budget

Keswick YHA (☎0845 371 9746; www.yha.org.uk; Station Rd; dm £15-35; ⏰reception 7am-11pm; 📶) A super YHA overlooking the river and park.

Ambleside YHA (☎0345 371 9620; www.yha.org.uk; Lake Rd; dm £18-32; P 📶) Halfway from Windermere to Ambleside; great for outdoor activities.

Great Langdale Campsite (NT; ☎015394-63862; www.nationaltrust.

org.uk/features/great-langdale-campsite; Great Langdale; sites £12-25, extra adult £6, pods £35-70; arrivals 3-7pm Sat-Thu, to 9pm Fri; P) Pitch a tent with views of the Langdale Pikes.

Wasdale Hall YHA (0845-371 9350; www.yha.org.uk; Wasdale Hall, Nether Wasdale; dm £13-30; reception 8-10am & 5-10.30pm; P) An ideal base for launching a Scafell Pike attempt.

Derwentwater Independent Hostel (017687-77246; www.derwentwater.org; Barrow House; dm £24, s & d £60, tr £66-75, q £83-96; P @) A former country house turned friendly Borrowdale hostel.

Black Sail YHA (0845-371 9680; www.yha.org.uk; dm £35; mid-Mar–Oct, check-in 5-9pm) Wild bothy in the hills above Ennerdale.

Best Midrange

Rum Doodle (015394-45967; www.rumdoodlewindermere.com; Sunny Bank Rd, Windermere Town; d £95-139; P) Imaginative, fun B&B in Windermere with a vintage feel.

Wasdale Head Inn (019467-26229; www.wasdale.com; s £59, d £118-130, tr £177; P) A remote inn crammed with hiking history.

Howe Keld (017687-72417; www.howekeld.co.uk; 5-7 The Heads; s £65-90, d £110-140; P) A boutique B&B base in Keswick.

Eltermere Inn (015394-37207; www.eltermere.co.uk; Elterwater; r £149-295; P) Handsome inn near the shores of Elterwater.

Punch Bowl Inn (015395-68237; www.the-punchbowl.co.uk; Crosthwaite; mains £15.95-24.50; noon-4pm & 5.30-8.30pm; P) Stylish rooms at an award-winning gastropub.

Halston Aparthotel (01228-210240; www.thehalston.com; 20-34 Warwick Rd; 1-bed apt £120-140, 2-bed apt £240-280; P) Sleek sleeps in central Carlisle.

Heritage Organisations

Membership of one of the UK's two large heritage organisations gets you free admission for some of the area's big-ticket sights, including Hill Top, Wordsworth House and the Beatrix Potter Gallery. Even better, it gets you free parking at the Trust's numerous car parks.

National Trust (NT; www.nationaltrust.org.uk) A charity protecting historic buildings and land with scenic importance across England and Wales. Annual membership is £69 (discounts for under-26s and families). A Touring Pass allows free entry to NT properties for one/two weeks (one person £31/36, two people £55/66, family £61/77).

English Heritage (EH; www.english-heritage.org.uk) State-funded organisation responsible for numerous historic sites. Annual membership is £56 (couples and seniors get discounts). An Overseas Visitors Pass allows free entry to most sites for nine/16 days for £33/39 (couples £57/67, families £62/72).

Best Top End

Forest Side (015394-35250; www.theforestside.com; Keswick Rd; r incl full board £230-400; P Wi-Fi) All the boutique spoils you could hope for.

Another Place, The Lake (017684-86442; www.another.place; Watermillock; r £230-290, f £345-385; P Wi-Fi) Trendy, outdoors-focused hotel on Ullswater.

Gilpin Hotel (015394-88818; www.gilpinlodge.co.uk; Crook Rd; r £275-465; P) Posh suites and a Michelin-starred restaurant near Windermere.

Brimstone Hotel (015394-38062; www.brimstonehotel.co.uk; Langdale Estate, Great Langdale; r £340-520; P) The ultimate in Lakeland lodge luxury.

Cottage in the Wood (017687-78409; www.thecottageinthewood.co.uk; Braithwaite; d £130-220; restaurant 6.30-9pm Tue-Sat; P Wi-Fi) Super restaurant and sophisticated dining near Whinlatter Forest.

Daffodil Hotel (015394-63550; www.daffodilhotel.co.uk; d £145-260, ste £180-340; P Wi-Fi) A relaxing, smart, modern hotel not far from Grasmere.

Arriving in the Lake District

Windermere

Trains direct run from Oxenholme and Kendal to Windermere Town. Buses leave regularly from the Windermere train station for most towns and villages in the Lake District, including Ambleside, Grasmere, Keswick and Coniston.

Carlisle

The city's airport is 8 miles northeast, and has direct flights to/from London Southend, Dublin and Belfast. Carlisle's train station is in the middle of the city centre. To book a taxi, call **Radio Taxis** (01228-527575) or **Cumbria Cabs** (01228-899599).

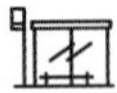

Getting Around

Bicycle

Cycling is a popular and fun way to explore the Lake District, but you will have to be prepared to deal with some hills. Some buses have spaces for carrying bikes, but check with local tourist offices before you travel.

Boat

There are round-the-lake ferry services on **Windermere** (www.cumbria.gov.uk/roads-transport/highways-pavements/windermereferry.asp; car/bicycle/pedestrian £4.40/1/50p; every 20 min 6.50am-9.50pm Mon-Fri, 9.10am-9.50pm Sat & Sun Mar-Oct, to 8.50pm Nov-Feb), Coniston Water, Ullswater and Derwentwater. Windermere also has cruises and a cross-lake ferry service.

Bus

The main bus operator is **Stagecoach** (www.

stagecoachbus.com). Services on most routes are reduced in winter. You can download timetables from the Stagecoach website or the Cumbria County Council website (www.cumbria.gov.uk). Bus timetables are also available from tourist offices.

Useful services:

Bus 555 (Lakeslink) Lancaster to Keswick, stopping at all the main towns, including Windermere and Ambleside.

Bus 505 (Coniston Rambler) Kendal, Windermere, Ambleside and Coniston.

Bus X4/X5 Penrith to Workington via Troutbeck, Keswick and Cockermouth.

Car & Motorcycle

Traffic can be heavy during peak season and holiday weekends. Many Cumbrian towns use timed parking permits for on-street parking, which you can pick up free from local shops and tourist offices.

If you're driving to the Lake District, National Trust membership is a good idea, as it means you can park for free at all of the National Trust's car parks (which otherwise charge extortionately high rates).

Essential Information

Accessible Travel

With many old buildings and plenty of challenging terrain, the Lake District often is not the easiest place for people with disabilities – especially those with reduced mobility. Having said that, efforts are being made to open up the key sights as much as possible, and also to create wheelchair-friendly walks such as the 48 **Miles without Stiles Routes** (www.lakedistrict.gov.uk/visiting/thingstodo/walking/mileswithout-stiles).

Download Lonely Planet's free Accessible Travel guides from http://lptravel.to/AccessibleTravel.

Useful organisations include:

Lake District Access for All (www.lakedistrict.gov.uk/visiting/planyourvisit/accessforall) Useful advice from the National Park Authority on accessible sights.

Disability Rights UK (www.disabilityrightsuk.org) Published titles include a *Holiday Guide*. Other services include a key for 7000 public disabled toilets across the UK.

Good Access Guide (www.goodaccessguide.co.uk)

Tourism For All (www.tourismforall.org.uk)

Business Hours

Standard business hours are as follows:

Banks 9am-4pm or 5pm Monday to Friday, 9am-12.30pm Saturday.

Post Offices 9am-5.30pm Monday to Friday, 9am-12.30pm Saturday. Main branches to 5pm.

Pubs Generally 11am-11pm, city pubs sometimes open to midnight or 1pm on Friday and Saturday.

Restaurants Lunch noon-3pm, dinner from 7pm-10pm.

Shops & Supermarkets 9am-5.30pm Monday to Saturday, 10am-4pm Sunday.

Discount Cards

Several travel passes are available.

Lakes Day Ranger (adult/child/family £23/11.50/45) The best-value one-day ticket, allowing a day's unlimited travel on trains and buses in the Lake District. It also includes a boat cruise on Windermere, 10% discount on the steam railways and 20% discount on the Coniston Launch, Keswick Launch and Ullswater Steamers.

Cumbria Day Ranger (adult/child £43/21.50) This pass provides one day's train travel in Cumbria and parts of Lancashire, North Yorkshire, Northumberland and Dumfries and Galloway.

Central Lakes Dayrider (adult/child/family £8.30/6.20/23) This pass covers Stagecoach buses around Bowness, Ambleside, Grasmere, Langdale and Coniston; it includes buses 599, 505 and 516. For an extra £4/2 per adult/child you can add a boat cruise on Windermere or Coniston.

Keswick & Honister Dayrider (adult/child/family £8.30/6.20/23) Covers buses from Keswick through Borrowdale, Buttermere, Lorton and the Whinlatter Forest Park.

North West Megarider Gold (per week £28) Covers seven days' travel on all Stagecoach buses operating in Lancashire, Merseyside, Cumbria, West Cheshire and Newcastle.

Electricity

Type G
230V/50Hz

Internet Access

Many hotels, B&Bs, restaurants, cafes and tourist office in Cumbria offer wi-fi access (usually, but not always, free of charge).

There are relatively few internet cafe's, although most town libraries offer internet access at public terminals.

Money

ATMs

- ATMs (usually called 'cash machines' in England) are common in most larger towns in the Lake District; some local shops and a few pubs also have them.
- Cash withdrawals from some ATMs may be subject to a small charge, but most are free.
- If you're not from the UK, your home bank will likely charge you a fee (and not-great exchange rate) for withdrawing money overseas.

Cash

The currency of Britain is the pound sterling (£). Paper money (notes) comes in £5, £10, £20 and £50 denominations. Some shops don't accept £50 notes because fakes circulate.

Other currencies are very rarely accepted, except at some gift shops in London, which may take euros, US dollars, yen and other major currencies.

Credit & Debit Cards

Visa and MasterCard are widely accepted in England, except at some smaller B&Bs, which take cash or cheque only. Other credit cards, including Amex, are not so widely accepted. Most businesses will assume your card is 'Chip and PIN' enabled (using a PIN instead of signing). If it isn't, you should be able to sign instead, but some places may not accept your card.

Changing Money

You can also change money at many post offices – very handy in country areas, and exchange rates are fair.

Tipping

In England you're not obliged to tip if the service or food was unsatisfactory (even if it's been automatically added to your bill as a 'service charge').

Restaurants Around 10% in restaurants and teahouses with table service, 15% at smarter restaurants. Tips may be added to your bill as a 'service charge'. Not compulsory.

Pubs & Bars Not expected if you order drinks (or food) and pay at the bar; usually 10% if you order at the table and your meal is brought to you.

Taxis Usually 10%, or rounded up to the nearest pound, especially in London.

Weather

The Lake District's weather is infamously unpredictable. While it's always worth checking the latest forecast, you should be prepared for all eventualities.

The Lake District Weatherline (www.lake-district.gov.uk/weatherline) provides a five-day forecast courtesy of the National Park Authority (NPA), while the Mountain Weather Information Service (www.mwis.org.uk) provides a downloadable forecast for the Lake District.

The Met Office (www.met-office.gov.uk) provides tailored forecasts for specific areas; you can search by region or input a town or postcode.

Public Holidays

Holidays for the whole of Britain:

New Year's Day 1 January

Easter March/April (Good Friday to Easter Monday inclusive)

May Day First Monday in May

Spring Bank Holiday Last Monday in May

Summer Bank Holiday Last Monday in August

Christmas Day 25 December

Boxing Day 26 December

Safe Travel

Though they're comparatively small in world terms, the Lakeland fells can still be dangerous if you're not properly prepared. Trails are often rough, exposed and indistinct, signposts are few and far between, and the weather can change without warning.

Hiking Safely

- Research your route well in advance, and choose a route that's within your abilities. 'Cragfast' – stuck – hikers are one of the most common call-outs for rescue teams.
- Always carry a proper map and compass, and know how to use them. A day spent brushing up navigational skills with a local walking company is recommended.
- Wear proper waterproof hiking boots (ideally with high sides to avoid sprained ankles).
- Dress in breathable layers for insulation, with a waterproof rainshell (Gore-Tex or equivalent) to keep you dry and allow moisture to evaporate from your skin.
- On the day of your walk, let someone know your intended route and estimated time of return. Check the weather forecast before you set out and ask around for advice about any new hazards that may have cropped up along the route.
- It's worth carrying a mobile phone in case of emergencies, but reception is notoriously patchy.

Hiking Equipment Check List

- Topographical hiking map and compass
- At least 2L of water per person
- Spare padded socks
- Layered clothing (base, mid-layer and fleece)
- Breathable jacket (Gore-Tex or equivalent)
- Waterproof trousers
- Food, trail snacks and energy bars
- First aid kit and sunscreen
- Mobile phone
- Gaiters (useful on muddy trails)

Tourist Information

The national park's main visitor centre is at **Brockhole** (015394-46601; www.brockhole.co.uk; 10am-5pm), just outside Windermere, and there are tourist offices in **Windermere** (015394-46499; www.windermereinfo.co.uk; Victoria St; 8.30am-5.30pm), **Bowness** (0845 901 0845; bownesstic@lake-district.gov.uk; Glebe Rd; 9.30am-5.30pm), **Ambleside** (015394-32582; tic@thehubofambleside.com; Central Bldgs, Market Cross; 9am-5pm), **Keswick** (017687-72645; www.keswick.org; Moot Hall, Market Pl; 9.30am-4.30pm;), **Coniston** (015394-41533; www.conistontic.org; Ruskin Ave; 9.30am-4.30pm Mon-Sat, 10am-2pm Sun) and **Carlisle** (01228-598596; www.discovercarlisle.co.uk; Greenmarket; 9.30am-5pm Mon-Sat, 10.30am-4pm Sun).

All have information on local sights, activities, accommodation and public transport and can help with accommodation bookings.

Behind the Scenes

Send Us Your Feedback

We love to hear from travellers – your comments help make our books better. We read every word, and we guarantee that your feedback goes straight to the authors. Visit **lonelyplanet.com/contact** to submit your updates and suggestions.

Note: We may edit, reproduce and incorporate your comments in Lonely Planet products such as guidebooks, websites and digital products, so let us know if you don't want your comments reproduced or your name acknowledged. For a copy of our privacy policy visit lonelyplanet.com/privacy.

Oliver's Thanks

A big thank you to all the many people who helped me and provided guidance and suggestions during my research in the Lake District, Cumbria and beyond. Special thanks to Cliff Wilkinson for giving me the gig; to everyone in-house at Lonely Planet; to Susie and Gracie Berry for long-distance emails; and to Rosie Hillier for keeping the home fires burning.

Acknowledgements

Cover photograph: Grasmere in autumn, Lake District, Nadia Isakova/Alamy ©

Photographs pp30-1 (clockwise from bottom left): D K Grove/Shutterstock©; Pecold/Shutterstock©; David Goddard/Getty Images©

This Book

This 1st edition of Lonely Planet's *Pocket Lake District* guidebook was researched and written by Oliver Berry. This guidebook was produced by the following:

Destination Editor
Clifton Wilkinson

Senior Product Editor
Genna Patterson

Regional Senior Cartographer
Mark Griffiths

Product Editor
Ross Taylor

Book Designer
Michael Weldon

Assisting Editors Imogen Bannister, Charlotte Orr

Assisting Cartographer
Rachel Imeson

Cover Researcher
Naomi Parker

Thanks Liz Heynes, Andi Jones, Kate Kiely, Martine Power

Index

See also separate subindexes for:
Eating p156
Drinking p157
Entertainment p157
Shopping p157

Sights 000
Map Pages **000**

Sights 000
Map Pages **000**

Notes

Our Writer

Oliver Berry

Oliver Berry is a writer and photographer from Cornwall. He has been writing for Lonely Planet for more than a decade, covering destinations from Cornwall to the Cook Islands and contributing to more than 30 guidebooks. He is also a regular contributor to many newspapers and magazines, including Lonely Planet's *Traveller.* His writing has won several awards, including *The Guardian* Young Travel Writer of the Year and the *TNT Magazine's* People's Choice Award. His latest work is published at www.oliverberry.com.

Published by Lonely Planet Global Limited
CRN 554153
1st edition – Apr 2019
ISBN 978 1 78701 761 0

10 9 8 7 6 5 4 3 2 1
Printed in Singapore